CONTENTS

D0376040

CONCEPT OF THE ROUTE AND USING THE BOOK

Most walks in the Lake District, and for that matter elsewhere, are completed within a day. These routes tend to be circuitous in nature, with the walkers usually returning to their starting location of a car park, a bus route or the place at which they happen to be staying overnight. When suitable transport is available, such as when the walking party have access to more than one car, or are supported by a coach, etc., they have more freedom to choose a linear type of route. In these circumstances the walking party may finish a hike many miles away from their original starting point, and they will have trekked continuously over new terrain for the entire walk.

The concept of adding these individual linear walks of convenient daily length together to form an attractive and demanding long-distance route has grown in popularity in recent years, particularly since the opening of the Pennine Way. Walkers are nowadays, in ever increasing numbers, attracted to these long distance routes and they obviously obtain immense pleasure and satisfaction in completing them within the time-frames they have set themselves. Most of the recognized long distance walks, however, do have a fairly rigidly defined single way, and although there are alternatives in certain sections of almost every route, in the main, there is usually limited scope for alternatives that cater specifically for the separate needs of a very wide spectrum of ages, abilities and personal preferences.

ARRANGEMENT

The Lakeland Round is a high-level, long-distance walking route consisting of several very flexible alternative ways for walkers of most age groups and of varying fitness and ability to really enjoy trekking over the fells and along the valleys of this rugged and magnificent mountain terrain. They will do this by selecting a

Above the clouds on Coniston Old Man

5

THE LAKELAND ROUND: MAIN ROUTE

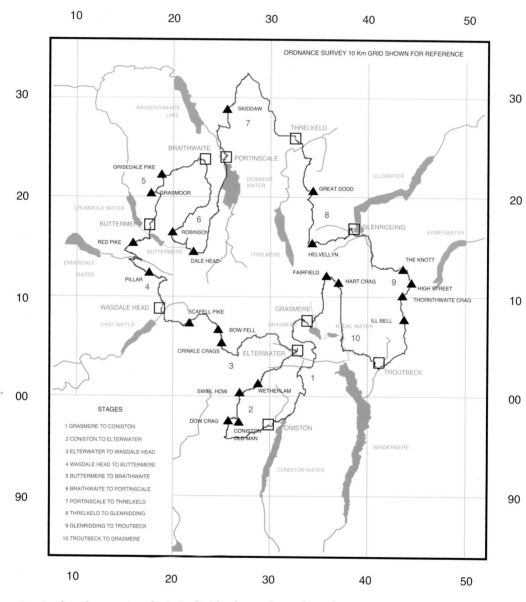

circuit that best suits their individual needs and preferences from a variety of alternatives described. Groups of walkers with mixed abilities may therefore split up each, or on any particular, day to follow two or more route variants, before they meet up again in the evening at the next planned overnight location. For most walkers the ideal route will be one that is demanding for them, but at the same time is well within their physical and mental capabilities, and as such the successful completion of their chosen route should give them immense satisfaction. Other walkers will have different priorities, and these will be reflected in the combination of alternatives they select for each separate stage of the route. Thus the precise walk undertaken will be unique to each walking party, but within a recognized, overall framework.

The walk was conceived to link together ten attractively located Lakeland villages or hamlets by means of an exploration of the high fells that would encompass the climbing of most of

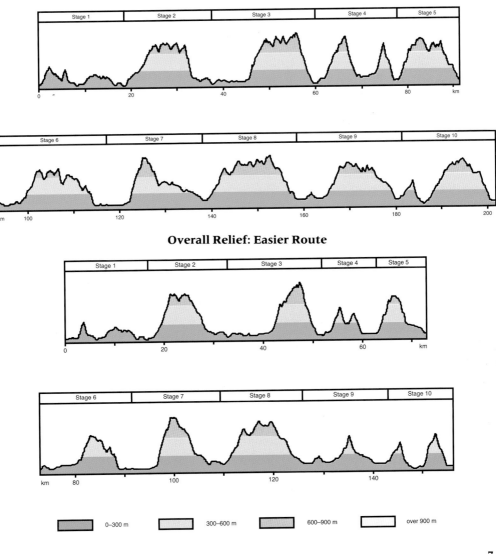

Overall Relief: Main Route

Overall Relief: Easier Route

0–300 m   300–600 m   600–900 m   over 900 m

the major mountain peaks, and of passing through all the different types of Lakeland scenery, including the rugged Borrowdale Volcanics and the more rounded Skiddaw Slates. The locations were selected on the main criterion that they possessed adequate overnight accommodation in a wide price-bracket, ranging from youth hostels to good-class, medium-sized hotels. Each location was chosen for its potential to provide several walking routes – of varying severity but all having interest and variety – to the next destination. Finally, each stage had to have alternatives that could be completed within daylight hours, at most times of the year, in variable weather conditions, by walkers possessing wide differences in ability and fitness. This latter constraint, in effect, meant that each main stage had to be limited to within a maximum distance of about 25 kilometres (15 miles), and a total height climbed of some 1,500 metres (5,000 feet), with several easier curtailments.

MAIN AND ALTERNATIVE ROUTES

To cater for the needs of powerful, but by no means super-human walkers, a main route is described for each stage. It is envisaged that the majority of experienced fell walkers will follow this main route. For those who wish to tackle an even more challenging itinerary, a number of optional extensions are provided for each stage, whenever this is both feasible and sensible. An easier route is also provided for each of the ten separate stages, with further curtailments also given for those who might find themselves in difficulties during any one particular stage. This could happen to any walker who may experience, for example, severely blistered toes and/or tummy trouble on the odd day or so. It would be a great pity if something like this jeopardized the completion of the entire walk for those who had to comply with a strict time deadline. The main and easier alternatives for each stage either cross over and/or use some identical sections, and therefore parts of both routes may, in many cases, be combined to provide further flexible variants of your own choice, and these may be mixed to provide walks of varying severity, stage by stage.

Grasmere is the advocated starting location for the walk, and there are two reasons for this choice. The first is that this is a popular tourist centre with extensive accommodation and other attractions, and it is relatively easy to reach by road. The second is that of all the ten stages, the one linking Grasmere to Coniston is the least demanding in physical terms, and this will allow you to become accustomed to the weight of the backpack, to generally acclimatize yourself and become fitter in preparation for the more difficult stages ahead. However, the walk may be commenced from any of the ten stopping places; Coniston makes a very acceptable alternative to Grasmere, particularly if you decide to complete The Round in an anti-clockwise direction. Indeed, the best starting location is simply the one that is most convenient for you.

Although the walk has been designed as a high-level, long-distance one to be completed within an acceptable ten-day period, there is no reason why the route cannot be completed over a considerable longer time-scale, running into weeks, months or even years. An intermediate to these extremes is to tackle two or more stages over, say, a weekend and to spend several of these enjoyably completing the round. There will, of course, be a few who will jog round the route and overtake the rest of us along the way, with their target set at reducing the existing record time for completing the route. Good luck to all of these dedicated, distance-devouring disciples.

The Lakeland Fells observed from the Moorhowe Road

ROUTE DESCRIPTIONS

The descriptive text for each stage of the route is set out in an identical format, and this is illustrated by route diagrams and by photographs. The diagrams include both a plan and an integrated cross-sectional relief that shows the profile of the walk. These diagrams have been generated by computer techniques, and are based on reference plots downloaded from The Ordnance Survey Outdoor Leisure Maps of The English Lakes 4 centimetres to 1 kilometre (2½ inches to 1 mile) − 1:25000 series. They are therefore mathematically accurate, although they are not intended to be a substitute for a map when following the route. The photographs are of two types, those taken when walking along the route, and those observing parts of the route from other vantage points. The majority of these photographs are of the main route. Camera symbols have been inserted in the plan diagram of the route indicating the position, and direction of take, of each photograph. There is also a distinctive number identifying each photograph, and this appears both next to the camera symbol in the plan diagram and also as part of the caption of each photograph, to facilitate identification. Each distinctive reference number has three components; these in turn indicate the walking stage concerned, whether the photograph primarily illustrates the main (M) or the easier (E) route variant, and finally the sequence of the photograph within each stage of the walk. Thus the photograph referenced 2M/3 is the third photograph along the main route of the second walking stage; 2M/4 is the next photograph illustrating the same stage of the walk, and so on.

A pertinent overview and statistics of each stage of the walk are provided in a summary layout at the start of each walking route chapter. These include a brief description of the starting location, a note on the landscape and features of interest, comments on footpaths and route finding, time allowances, distances to be walked, overall heights climbed and the names and heights of the principal peaks visited. This is followed by a description of the route variants for each walking stage.

The estimates of walking time include allowances for all stops including lunch. These have been calculated by allowing 1 hour to walk each 2½ miles, plus an allowance of a further 1 hour for every 2000 feet climbed, plus a further 1 hour for all stops, and a final adjustment of up to plus or minus ½ hour per stage to compensate for all other factors, such as difficulty of route finding, state of the paths, type of terrain, sections involving scrambling, etc. You will need to adjust these basic estimates to suit your own capability and speed-of-walking preferences.

Further chapters in the book cover such important considerations as clothing, equipment, nourishment and safety; the finding of suitable and convenient overnight accommodation, including a register of addresses and contact telephone numbers; and comprehensive statistics of the Round.

Bow Fell and The Band

MISCELLANEOUS

Abbreviations have been kept to a minimum and are used to avoid constant repetition of well-known, awkward compounded words. These are listed in Table 1, starting with familiar directional indicators and compass bearings.

TABLE 1 **ABBREVIATIONS**

L	left	WNW	west-north-west
R	right	NW	north-west
N	north	NNW	north-north-west
NNE	north-north-east	cm	centimetre(s)
NE	north-east	ft	feet
ENE	east-north-east	K-gate	kissing-gate
E	east	km	kilometre(s)
ESE	east-south-east	L-stile	ladder-stile
SE	south-east	m	metres
SSE	south-south-east	P-stile	post-stile
S	south	W-stile	wall-stile
SSW	south-south-west	MR	map reference
SW	south-west	OLM(s)	Outdoor Leisure Map(s)
WSW	west-south-west	OS	Ordnance Survey
W	west	YH	Youth Hostel

Dialect words and place names used are shown in Table 2.

TABLE 2 **DIALECT WORDS AND PLACE NAMES**

beck	stream
bield	sheltered or protected land
cairn	heap of stones, usually pointed
crag	steep rugged rock or peak
dale	valley
dub	pool
fell	hill or mountain
force	waterfall
ghyll/gill	watercourse in a ravine
hause	summit of narrow pass, col
how	rounded hill
knott	rocky outcrop
nab/neb	promontory
pike	pointed summit
rigg	ridge
scar	escarpment
scree	loose, shattered rock on mountain slope
tarn	small expanse of water
thwaite	clearing

No guide book is an adequate substitute for maps and a compass. Use the four Ordnance Survey Outdoor Leisure Maps 4, 5, 6, and 7, and Pathfinder Map 576 Caldbeck, scale 1:25000, and a reliable compass at all times when you are walking the Lakeland Round. Be sure that you know how to use this combination correctly.

All compass bearings have been given to the nearest 22½ degree point, e.g. N, NNE, NE etc. This is considered to be sufficiently accurate over the relatively short distances travelled between the taking of successive readings. Note that some Lakeland rocks contain minerals with magnetic properties and therefore certain compass bearings will not always be true; this is particularly prevalent in the vicinity of Bow Fell. Therefore take frequent bearings, particularly when the visibility is poor.

Lakeland artefacts are constantly changing; fences appear and disappear, K-gates replace L-stiles and vice-versa, additional waymarker signs appear, some signs get removed and so on. Therefore, should you notice isolated differences along the route from those described, presume that these have occurred since the book went to press, and proceed with confidence to the next feature described. Care has been taken to include some references where you can be absolutely sure that you are standing at the right spot without being confused by man-made features. Rely on these as your dominant guide.

The heights of the major fells have been given in both metric and imperial measurements extracted from relevant OS OLMs. There are some minor anomalies between the two sets of measurements that are not readily explained by rounding-off differences!

Finally, sometimes there is more than one version of the spelling of place names. In such instances the spelling that appears on the OS OLMs has been used, unless otherwise indicated.

CLOTHING, EQUIPMENT, NOURISHMENT AND SAFETY

EXPERTISE NEEDED

Based on the sound principle that prevention is better than cure, only walkers who have adequate experience of completing walks over challenging mountainous terrain of at least several full days' duration should attempt The Lakeland Round. It is considered essential that all groups of walkers who undertake this demanding, high-level walking route should have members in their party who are proficient in navigation, are able to read, interpret and anticipate changing weather patterns in mountainous terrain, are competent in administering basic first aid, including the prevention of mountain hyperthermia and dealing with the effects of heat. Additionally, they must be able to cope effectively with accident and illness situations, including mountain-rescue procedures, even though such eventualities are very rare indeed. Only very strong and vastly experienced walkers should attempt The Round in winter, and in these extreme conditions all members of the party should have received adequate training in snow and ice techniques, and they should know how to maintain security in such a hostile environment. The leader should always ensure that members in his/her party do not become separated.

FIRST AID

All leaders of walking groups should have attended recognized first-aid courses conducted under the auspices of St John Ambulance, the British Red Cross Society, or similar bodies, and all participants should be proficient in coping with such emergencies as absence of breath or pulse, clearing an obstructed airway, arresting severe bleeding, protecting an injured companion and also safely removing a victim from any life-threatening hazard.

SAFETY PRECAUTIONS

Safety precautions are aimed at cutting down risk to an absolute acceptable minimum. To start with, only venture onto the high fells well prepared, carrying detailed maps of the area, a reliable compass, and a torch; with a reserve of food and drink, adequately clothed, taking additional protective wearing clothing with you and in possession of an adequate first-aid kit. Additionally have a clear, but flexible, route plan in your mind, carefully conceived before you set out.

One very important factor to recognize is that English weather is notoriously capricious at *all* times of the year. No matter how pleasant the weather is at the start, ten days or more is a long time to spend in the mountains, so *always* err on the side of caution, and anticipate that weather conditions could change/ deteriorate significantly.

The most important common-sense precaution is to look where you are putting your feet! Additionally, when undertaking scrambling over craggy outcrops, always test that critical hand-holds will momentarily take your full weight in the event of this safeguard being needed.

Make a practice of taking frequent compass bearings, particularly in misty conditions, and work on the sound principle of always knowing where you are, within short distances.

Another sensible precaution is to inform the proprietors of the place that you stayed at overnight, and also those at the next intended port of call, if this has been decided.

GETTING HELP AFTER AN ACCIDENT

In the unlikely event of an incapacitating illness or an accident, the prime task becomes that of summoning expert help as quickly as possible. Before you attempt to do this render any first aid that is essential, make your companion as warm as possible and leave as much food and drink as you can. Before leaving, firmly attach an accident report to the victim. All members of the party who either are not needed to stay with the victim or go for help, should be evacuated.

With a larger party at least two members should always go for help. First, take an exact map reference of the spot, memorize the distinctive land features, make a note of the time, and then find the nearest form of habitation to contact the emergency services.

The emergency signal is six short blasts on a whistle, or flashes with a torch, repeated at minute intervals. (The answering acknowledgement is three such return signals.)

CLOTHING, EQUIPMENT AND NOURISHMENT

A comprehensive listing follows of the items I would consider taking with me on The Round, my final selection being dependent upon weather conditions.

On no account attempt to burden yourself with a load that is so heavy and cumbersome that you are not able to enjoy the walk to the full. Try to limit the weight of your filled rucksack to, for male walkers 25 pounds or so, depending upon your physique; with the ladies in the party carrying some 5 pounds less per person. A camera, binoculars, and when necessary, an ice axe and crampons will add further weight. In any event, these sensible weight constraints will still probably imply that you have to carry a load at least twice as heavy as that required for a day's walk. In preparing for The Round it is advisable to test the appropriateness of the weight of your intended load by carrying a similarly filled rucksack on, say, two or more consecutive full-day walks to see how you get on with this.

It is essential to wear robust but comfortable, well-worn boots that provide adequate waterproof protection. Fortunately, nowadays, there is a wide range of reliable makes to choose from.

TABLE 3   **CLOTHING**

'Normal' weather

Breathable waterproofs	2 changes of underwear
Ultra-fleece jacket	2 changes of socks
Breeches	2 extra shirts
Woollen ski hat or balaclava*	Clothing for evenings
Fine woollen mitts	Handkerchiefs
Thermal underwear*	Spare bootlaces

Extras for hot summer weather:

Shorts	Sun-hat

Extras for extreme winter weather:

Additional sweater	Thermal ski mitts
Storm gear	Waterproof gaiters

*Unlikely to be selected in conjunction with the additional items suggested for hot summer weather

CAUTIONARY NOTE: On no account should denim-type jeans be worn, as when wet they can become extremely uncomfortable, and, more importantly, in such conditions body heat-loss through them is considerable. This will increase significantly the risk of exposure.

TABLE 4 **EQUIPMENT**

All seasons:

Money and cheque book
  (incl. coins for phone)
Credit cards
Stamps & postcards
Identification
Wallet
Rucksack (incl. waterproof
liner)
Maps
Compass
Watch
Guide book
Head-torch
Spare bulb & batteries
Whistle
Swiss army knife
Thermos flask
Water bottle
Food container
Survival bag
Notebook and pen
Camera and lenses
Films
Spare camera batteries

Binoculars
String
Needle and thread
Spare buttons
Toilet paper
Toiletries
Washing powder
First-aid kit:
  assorted plasters and strip
  dumbel sutures
  bandages, including:
    triangular
    elastic (for sprains)
  wound dressing
  chiropody felt
  antiseptic wipes
  insect repellent
  surgical spirits
  cotton wool pads
  painkiller tablets
  scissors
  safety pins
  luggage labels

Extras for hot summer weather

Sun-glasses

Sun-cream & lip-salve

Extras for extreme winter weather:

Ski goggles
Ice axe

Crampons

TABLE 5 **NOURISHMENT**

'Normal' weather:

Food
Drink
Glucose tablets

Chocolate
Boiled sweets

Extras for hot summer weather:

Additional cold drink

Extras for extreme winter weather:

Additional hot drink

Emergency rations

Stage 1
GRASMERE
to
CONISTON

Photograph: Looking down on
Grasmere from Silver How

STAGE 1 GRASMERE TO CONISTON

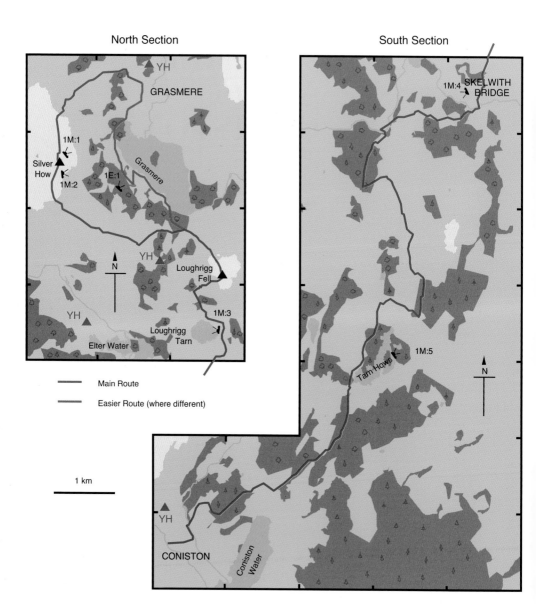

North Section

South Section

YH
GRASMERE

SKELWITH
BRIDGE
1M:4

1M:1

Silver
How
1M:2
1E:1

Grasmere

N

YH
Loughrigg
Fell

YH
1M:3

Loughrigg
Tarn
Elter Water

Tarn Hows
1M:5

N

—— Main Route

—— Easier Route (where different)

1 km

YH

CONISTON

Coniston
Water

TIME ALLOWANCE
Main Route: 7½ hours
Easier Route: 6½ hours

STARTING LOCATION

Grasmere village, just off A591, N of Grasmere Lake.

OLM 7/MR 336076.

Car park: Broadgate Meadow – holds about 80 cars.

Start walk from village square.

OVERVIEW/INTEREST

Two craggy fells of modest height and several quiet waters amongst forest scenery.

Views of several surrounding major peaks, including the Langdale Pikes and the Coniston Fells.

Abundant wildlife, including that associated with bog-pools.

Stretches of well-maintained farm land.

Grasmere Lake, Loughrigg Tarn, Skelwith Force and Tarn Hows are visited.

FOOTPATHS

Good and certain for most of the way with few boggy stretches.

No appreciable erosion, apart from the ascent and part of the descent from Loughrigg Fell.

Route finding rather complicated in places across the lower, inhabited ground.

Statistics	Main route		Easier route	
	Km	**Miles**	**Km**	**Miles**
Distance walked	19.5	12.1	17.5	10.9
	M	**Feet**	**M**	**Feet**
Height climbed	840	2750	600	1970
Principal Peaks	**M**	**Feet**	**M**	**Feet**
Silver How	395	1292	—	—
Loughrigg Fell	335	1101	335	1101

Stage 1 Grasmere to Coniston

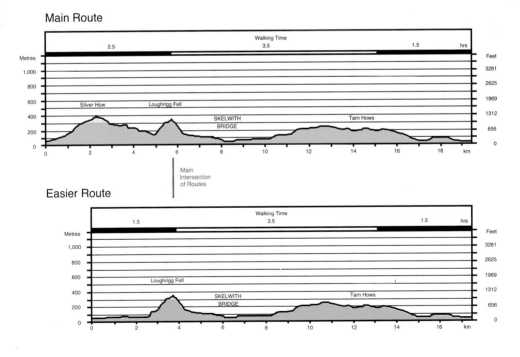

MAIN ROUTE   *(Allow 7½ hours)*

1M:1 Looking down on Grasmere nestling below Fairfield

The way to Loughrigg Fell   *(Allow 2½ hours)*

Leave the village square along the lane near Heaton Cooper's studio that leads NW. This departure is signed 'Public foothpath – Score Crag – Silver How'. The way winds up through parkland, skirting Allan Bank on your L, to reach two attractive cottages. From here the (now enclosed) path climbs more steeply, before a grassy way is accessed that twists up the open fellside to the juniper-bush fringed skyline above. The path then bears L along a less steep gradient before a rocky gully, somewhat concealed, is crossed down on your L. Pass a single guiding cairn to your R before walking along a grassy track that first leads SW, and then climbs up a comfortable incline, to attain the final, steeper, craggy slopes of Silver How.

Silver How commands extensive views in all directions, and in clear weather the high peaks of Bow Fell, Langdale Pikes, Helvellyn, Fairfield, Wetherlam, Pike of Blisco and Crinkle Crags are visible from its summit area.

Depart from Silver How to the sw, initially heading towards Wetherlam, in good weather silhouetted on the far horizon. There are several grassy ways down along the falling terrain, but the objective here is to keep to the higher ground as it veers se, sweeping round to your l, to attain, by surrendering only minimum height, the craggy spur ahead in the vicinity of Spedding Crag and Dow Bank. Veer eastwards, and follow the undulating higher contours of this ridge over Huntingstile Crag, before selecting the path that leads between Hammerscar Plantation and Redbank Wood down to the minor road at Red Bank (MR 340056). One treat along this stretch is a large bog-pool that attracts several varieties of dragonfly during hot summer days.

Cross the road and continue downhill towards Grasmere Lake along the track, virtually opposite, through Deer Bolts Wood. This leads to a National Trust Lake District Appeal collection point. Turn R here and climb up the steep, stony path by veering R again from the terrace, to gain the summit of Loughrigg Fell. Two fine views from here is the one northwards across Grasmere Lake towards Dunmail Raise, and the other southwards beyond Windermere. There are also new sightings to the E, including Red Screes, the impressive Ill Bell spur and Wansfell Pike towering above Ambleside.

1M:2 Grasmere and Rydal Water

The way to Tarn Hows   *(Allow 3½ hours)*

Leave the trigonometric point to the SE, and then turn abruptly R to descend a gully along a cairned, grassy path that leads through extensive bracken. (Avoid a narrower track leading off to the L, which presents a more complicated route down.) Some erosion will be encountered during the descent, and there are recently seeded areas undertaken to control the worst of this. Turn L at the bottom and proceed along the path towards Loughrigg Tarn. Pass through the first gate on your R, drop down to the driveway below, near 'The How', and veer L along this as it leads round Loughrigg Tarn at an elevated height.

The views across the tarn towards the Langdale Pikes are superb, particularly in June when the surface is smothered in a profusion of white water lilies, and water hens are busily feeding their chicks. It is well worth the short detour to visit the southern shoreline of these placid waters.

1M:3 Loughrigg Tarn and the Langdale Pikes

The driveway leads to a gate, after which turn R up the lane, passing 'Dillygarth' residence. Then in quick succession turn L, then R and then L again along the profusion of lanes and minor roads, to select the one that leads most directly, steeply down to Skelwith Bridge. A track heads W from here through the slate works to Skelwith Force, less than a ½ km (⅓ mile) away. The modest drop of these falls is nevertheless quite spectacular after heavy rain, and a visit is recommended.

1M:4 All eyes trained on Skelwith Force

Afterwards, leave Skelwith Bridge along the main A593 Ambleside to Coniston road, using this to cross the river Brathay. Ignore the first path on your R that leads only to a dead end at Skelwith Force, and beyond Ivy Cottage select the next footpath on your R, signed 'Colwith Bridge'. Follow the obvious route along part of The Cumbria Way to Park Farm and pass between the farm buildings. Inserted in the wall of a barn on your left is a rectangular stone slab on which are inscribed six different alphabets. The origins of this relic are obscure but it is thought to be the work of an apprentice stonemason. Continue westwards along the path following the directional arrowhead signs to Low Park. This residence is passed to your R, after which the way is through an iron turnstile.

AUTHOR'S NOTE: At Park Farm and Low Park there are private drives on the L that lead to the main road – they do not need to be accessed, and the privacy of these lanes should be respected.

The clear path next meanders round a pleasant grassy fellside before descending steeply beneath trees to the side of the beck below. A short distance further on, the minor road from Elterwater is reached near MR 331030. A National Trust sign opposite indicates a L turn up the road, and within 100 paces, after the road bends uphill to the R, select the path on your R. This leads downhill to a gate and is signed to Coniston. The way then continues SW between enclosing walls before it crosses a small watercourse by way of a wooden bridge. Beyond another gate, take the branch path on the L, again signed to Coniston. From here a broad path leads uphill to the S through a forest that is predominantly coniferous. This is Tongue Intake Plantation.

The obvious way continues S to emerge from the forest about ½ km (⅓ mile) further on. (Note this newish path is not shown on older editions of the OLM). Pass through a gap in a stone wall ahead and turn L along the surfaced lane. This will bring you to the main A593 Ambleside to Coniston road at MR 329022 (signed High Park). Cross the main road on a L diagonal, and walk along the grassy footpath directly ahead as it winds uphill before veering to the R to resume a SSE direction. Beyond a gate, revealing views open up to your L across the Langdale Valley and Elter Water, of the compact Fairfield Horseshoe and stately Helvellyn grouping.

Keep to the main path beside a stone wall on your L, as the land falls, before a small watercourse is crossed. The way is then uphill once more as the path veers to the R. Along here, in clear weather, the most superb views may be observed of the giant cradle of encircling high fells. These massive profiles include Wetherlam, Pike of Blisco, Crinkle Crags, Bow Fell and the Langdale Pikes. Towards the tip of the walled fellside, and immediately past a gate, pass through a gap to your L in the stone wall. The correct way here is indicated by white arrow-head markers. Next veer to the R, walking up the fell along a grassy path. In a short distance your path connects with a bridleway, and you turn R along this at MR 334020.

Beyond is Low Arnside that you pass above to the E. Within 1 km (⅔ mile) from here the bridleway enters, by way of a lower fork, the densely conifer forested area of The Iron Keld Plantation. A clear path leads down through this to a walled lane that you turn R along to emerge from under the canopy of trees. At the bottom of the slope The Cumbria Way footpath is re-engaged, and a L-stile on your L is climbed to enter the National Trust Land surrounding Tarn Hows. From here good footpaths are used to walk southwards round either side of the tarn before scaling the modest heights at the S tip of the tarn. You will then

be rewarded with quite splendid views down over the irregularly indented waters, and westwards towards the Coniston Fells
and NW to the Langdale Pikes.

The way to Coniston   *(Allow 1½ hours)*

Afterwards, make for the recently enlarged National Trust Car
Park situated to the SW of the tarn, and exit by the track leading
off from the SE corner of this to gain access to the forest trails
that will lead you SE down through Hill Fell Plantation, to
emerge at MR 318984, near to the junction of the B5285 road
and the single track lane from Tarn Hows. The descent through
the forest is delightful, and there are many species of coniferous
and broad-leaved trees and ground foliage to be observed along
the way.

Cross the road and select the newly constructed National Trust
footpath opposite that leads to the road near Boon Crag. Turn R
and proceed through the timber yard, and then up the track to
Boon Crag farm. When the track veers further uphill to the R,
locate a P-stile on your L and take the grassy path on the far side
of this. The way then leads over rising ground to the densely
forested hillock of Guards Wood.

White-topped, wooden marker posts indicate the route
through this enchanting wooded area, and this eventually leads
down in a semi-circle to your R, to an exit P-stile. Beyond this a
field is crossed on a downwards diagonal as your way passes
through a thick crop of gorse bushes. These present a profusion
of yellows and ochres in May, and also to a lesser extent in late
summer.

Continue downhill, once again making use of part of The
Cumbria Way footpath, and cross Yewdale Beck at Shepherd
Bridge to reach a minor road round Coniston village. Turn L
down this lane, and a final R turn onto the B5285 road will take
you to the centre of the village.

EXTENSIONS FOR STRONG WALKERS
For very strong and experienced walkers it is feasible to reach
Coniston by way of the Langdale Pikes! Two equally demanding
possibilities exist, one from the summit of Silver How westwards
along the undulating ridge of Lang How, and Castle How (Little
and Great) to the high ground of Blea Rigg, and the other to the
same general area but direct from Grasmere via Easedale,
Sourmilk Gill, Easedale Tarn and Belles Knott. From Blea Rigg,
accessed by either variant, Sergeant Man and the Langdale Pikes
are within easy walking distance. There are a variety of ways in

1M:5 Reflections in a
bog pool near Tarn
Hows

which walkers can then arrive at Stickle Tarn, with extremes of straight down the direct ascent from Blea Rigg, to visiting the summits of Sergeant Man, Pavey Ark and Harrison Stickle.

From Stickle Tarn descend by the newer path by the side of Stickle Ghyll, and head for the large camp site at the head of Great Langdale Valley at MR 286057. Good paths then lead southwards through the pass connecting the two Langdale valleys, along the w shore of Blea Tarn, and down by the side of Blea Moss, to connect with the road over Wrynose. Turn E here and walk down the road past Castle How to Fell Foot. Turn R and cross Fell Foot Bridge, proceed beyond Bridge End and then take the track that veers S up the fellside, leaving Atkinson Coppice on your L. Continue S down to High and then Low Tilberthwaite.

Cross Yewdale Beck and, beyond the adjacent car park, turn R up the steps and path through the quarry spoils. Your way now is along the narrow paths that wind up the fells to reach the pass between Furness Fells and Yewdale Fells. Walk over Hole Rake, and this leads to your final descent to the wide rutted track by the side of Church Beck. Follow this down into Coniston. (Some walk for the first day and probably only really suitable for those with the stamina of fell-runners!)

1E:1 Looking across Grasmere Lake towards Great Rigg

A less demanding extension is to first follow the prescribed main route to the N of Tarn Hows, but at MR 332007 instead of turning L over the P-Stile, continue northwards along The Cumbria Way route to arrive at the main A593 road at Oxen Fell High Cross. (There is an obvious short-circuit here by way of the path besides the main road from High Park.) Use the lane diagonally opposite to reach High Oxen Fell Farm, continue beyond, and with the buildings of Hodge Close visible, turn L to pass above the spectacular remains of several deep abandoned quarries. Continue along obvious paths to reach the road at Holme Ground. Turn L here. Take the second footpath on your R, and follow the signed paths to reach the car park at Tilberthwaite making use of the stony bank of Yewdale Beck and crossing the stream by means of the road bridge. From here use the directions given in the first suggested extension to arrive at Coniston.

EASIER ROUTE   *(Allow 6½ hours)*

The way to Loughrigg Fell   *(Allow 1½ hours)*

Start by walking up the road towards Elterwater over Red Bank, and after about 1½ km (1 mile), just past the side lane on the R that leads to Hunting Stile, take the path off on your L that descends to the W shoreline of Grasmere Lake. Follow the now established path round the shore to reach the southern most tip of the lake. The views across the waters towards Great Rigg and the other high fells leading to Fairfield are superb, with on many occasions, this impressive panorama also being reflected on the calm surface of the lake. Next climb up one of the steep paths to your R, where after a short exertion, you will cross Loughrigg Terrace and then a little further up connect with the main route at MR 344056. Thereafter, use the main route to reach the summit of Loughrigg Fell and from here continue along the main route to Coniston.

FURTHER CURTAILMENT

The prescribed easier route has been selected as a relatively undemanding start to a challenging long-distance, high-level walking route round the Lakeland Fells. Those walkers who find this alternative route difficult are inevitably going to encounter more serious problems on the following more severe stages of the route. Therefore, no further curtailments are considered appropriate at this juncture.

Stage 2

CONISTON
to
ELTERWATER

Photograph: Looking towards
Wetherlam and Elterwater

STAGE 2 CONISTON TO ELTERWATER

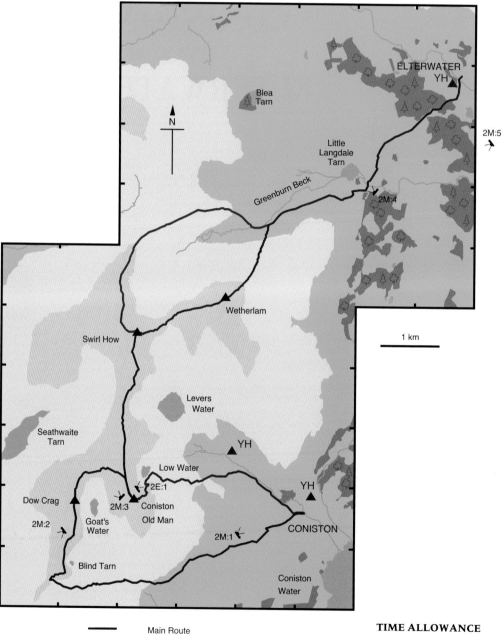

Main Route

Easier Route (where different)

TIME ALLOWANCE
Main Route: 8 hours
Easier Route: 7 hours

STARTING LOCATION
Coniston village, on A593, 1 km (⅔ mile) w of
Coniston Water, near top end of lake.
OLM 6/MR 303976.
Large car and coach park.
Start walk on lane signed 'Footpath to Old Man
– Walna Scar & Seathwaite', which is off the
A593, across Church Beck.

OVERVIEW/INTEREST
First the undulating, craggy, terrain along the
Walna Scar Road; then the high Coniston Fells
are penetrated.
Peaks climbed (on the main route) include Dow
Crag, Coniston Old Man, Swirl How and
Wetherlam.
Highlights include views of the Scafell Massif
and Dow Crag.

FOOTPATHS
Footpaths are still surprisingly good considering
the heavy, continuous usage they have to
endure.
Some patchy erosion, particularly near the top
of Coniston Old Man, and also during the
descent from Wetherlam.
No significant wet or boggy patches.
Route finding is relatively straightforward.

Statistics	Main route		Easier route	
	Km	**Miles**	**Km**	**Miles**
Distance walked	19.4	12.0	16.1	10.0
	M	**Feet**	**M**	**Feet**
Height climbed	1210	3970	950	3120
Principal Peaks	**M**	**Feet**	**M**	**Feet**
Dow Crag	778	2555	–	–
Coniston Old Man	803	2635	803	2635
Swirl How	802	2630	802	2630
Wetherlam	762	2502	–	–
Great Carrs	–	–	785	2575

Stage 2 Coniston to Elterwater

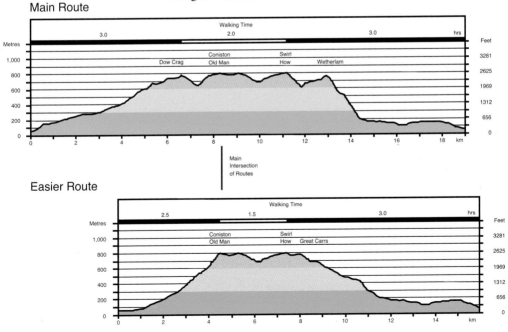

35

MAIN ROUTE   *(Allow 8 hours)*

The way to Dow Crag   *(Allow 3 hours)*

Walk up lane signed 'Footpath to Old Man . . .'. The first part of the way is exceptionally steep, until the lane snakes up the more open fellside along a less demanding gradient. Here fine views open up across the slopes leading up to the high peaks of the Coniston Fells and behind you there are increasingly revealing aspects of the Fairfield group of mountains and the major easterly fells, including High Street. Part of Coniston Water is also visible.

The Walna Scar Road proper continues to gain height as it pleasantly threads its way westwards round the craggy southern slopes of the satellite crags of Coniston Old Man. Higher up, in clear weather, the outlines of Brown Pike and then Dow Crag come into view cradling the high cove below Goat's Water. At the junction of the ways, near a massive cairn, take the lower L path which leads wsw. Torver Beck is crossed at Cove Bridge, before the track climbs, twisting up the steeper, rocky terrain of Goatfoot Crags. Then the top of the pass across the Walna Scar ridge is reached. Over the crest of this brow is a revealing view of the beautiful Duddon Valley and its protective westerly mountains of Ulpha Fell, and the higher, more pointed Harter Fell.

2M:1 The snow-capped Easterly Fells seen from the Walna Scar road

2M:2 Looking south from Buck Pike towards the Duddon estuary

Turn uphill and climb NE to reach Brown Pike. From here a cairned, and well-trodden path, leads through a shallow hause, before climbing to the next rocky pinnacle of Buck Pike. One final climb with some scrambling up craggy slopes is required to attain the large volcanic boulders that form the erratic summit of Dow Crag: a truly majestic peak. On the way up, the tiny Blind Tarn, so named because no exit stream is visible, and further on the larger tarn of Goat's Water, come into view, way below on your R.

The panorama from the summit of Dow Crag on a clear day is breathtaking and if you are lucky The Isle of Man, the Bow Fell grouping, Skiddaw and Blencathra, Helvellyn and Fairfield, Coniston Old Man and Black Combe are all visible.

The way to Swirl How   *(Allow 2 hours)*

Start your descent from Dow Crag to the NNE, keeping to the higher ground of the connecting ridge. This spur of rock bends progressively to the E as the ground falls to Goat's Hawse. From

here be careful to keep to the main, better defined L-hand path as your route climbs, again in a broad sweep, to reach the summit ridge leading to Coniston Old Man. You will be competing for space with an infuriating watercourse up this stretch, particularly when swollen from prolonged rainy weather, before a diagonal R fork, ESE, leads to the flatter ground of the high-level route along the ridge ahead. This converging access point is located at MR 271981.

Turn R along the main ridge route and walk southwards to reach the summit of Coniston Old Man, a short distance above. The extensive summit area is comfortable, and the large rectangle of elevated stones there provides adequate shelter from strong winds blowing from most directions. This summit also houses a tall marker cairn and, on occasion, meteorological measuring equipment. There are two contrasting views to be enjoyed from this lofty mountain peak, one southwards taking in the lower fells which surround Coniston Water together with the flatter landscape of the Duddon estuary, and the other northwards to the mountains of the Central Fells with their vast array of competing high and irregular volcanic peaks. Features visible for the first time include the blue, copper-sulphate tinged Low Water, and the peaks of High Raise, the Fairfield Horseshoe, and the High Street grouping far away to the NE.

2M:3 The snow-covered Scafells observed from Coniston Old Man

Leave the summit along your approach route but do not descend towards Goat's Hawse; instead continue walking northwards along the broad band which connects Coniston Old Man with Little and Great How Crags by means of the narrow col of Levers Hawse. Many new sightings are possible along here including, in succession, two of the massive, craggy spurs leading to the summit of Wetherlam; Levers Water, Seathwaite Tarn, and the massive bulk of Grey Friar. From Great How Crags your path continues N along Swirl Band and over protruding hillocks to reach eventually the summit of Swirl How. This is marked with a symmetrically conical-shaped, large cairn which is very distinctive.

The magnificent array of well-known peaks to be observed from this commanding summit in favourable weather include Hard Knott Crags, the Scafells, Crinkle Crags and Bow Fell, Glaramara, Pike of Blisco, Skiddaw, the Langdale Pikes, High Raise and Sergeant Man, Blencathra and the Helvellyn and Fairfield configurations. If this is not enough, the diminishing remains of a crashed aircraft can be picked out on the barren, inhospitable slopes of Great Carrs to the NNW!

The way to Elterwater   *(Allow 3 hours)*

Descend from Swirl How along Prison Band, walking first ESE along a gently sloping path for a short distance, before veering E to scramble down the pinnacle ridge. The route down is well cairned and most of the individual short pitches have several alternative descent paths. The band leads to Swirl Hawse, and from here a steep rocky slope ENE connects with a traverse to the L, up a less severe slope. Then, a narrow but well-defined path is used that veers E to gain the summit of Wetherlam. This fell does not have a discrete and imposing summit area but it does provide new perspectives, weather conditions permitting, including views of Stickle Tarn, Elter Water and the mountain peaks of Grasmoor and Robinson.

Use the rocky spur of Wetherlam Edge for the descent, leaving the summit along the steeply falling path to the NE. Although the way down is clearly cairned, this steep, in parts quite badly eroded route of descent, demands care and in a few places there are some awkward bits of scrambling down several rocky chutes. When Birk Fell Hawse is reached (MR 293016), abandon the crest of the spur by selecting the less distinct path down to your L. This is marked by intermittent cairns, and in changing your direction of travel, temporarily to N, your rapid rate of descent is maintained.

39

The way takes you down steep grassy slopes, before the path veers to the R along a more gradual line of descent that resumes your walking NE once more. Keep going down and be careful to ignore all paths that you cross heading up the fellside. Eventually your steadfast NE line of descent will lead you towards a formidable stone wall crossing the fellside, ahead and to your R. Trim your final approach to arrive at this, where the wall connects with a wide gravel path down below, and adjacent to the course of Greenburn Beck.

Turn R along this path and use the P-stile to cross the stone wall. The track leads north-eastwards to two National Trust holiday cottages at Hall Garth, situated about 1½ km (1 mile) further down the valley. Beyond these, cross the River Brathay at Slater Bridge and follow the way signed to Elterwater over High Birk Howe. When the road through Little Langdale is reached turn L down it, and then almost immediately R uphill off it, to connect with the track via Dale End leading to Elterwater.

EXTENSIONS FOR STRONG WALKERS

The main route as described is a challenging one and as this scales most of the major peaks in the Coniston Fell grouping, opportunities for extending the walk without losing significant height are limited. Possibilities for powerful walkers are from Swirl How to visit also Great Carrs, and from there perhaps also even Grey Friar, before retracing your steps to Swirl How. From there you can then continue along the main route by descending Prison Band.

EASIER ROUTE   *(Allow 7 hours)*

The way to Coniston Old Man   *(Allow 2½ hours)*

Leave the village by the lane along the R side of Bridge House cafe, just across Church Beck, walking WNW. The way uphill leads past The Sun Hotel, turn R here, following which the lane brings you to a pathway that winds up the valley into the open fells. This is by way of Dixon Ground Farm at which you veer L through a gate, following the path signed to the YH. This route, formerly one leading to sweat and toil at the now abandoned mine and quarry workings ahead, winds pleasantly beside the beck below on your R, as its waters gurgle merrily downhill in a series of miniature cascades into small, deep catchment pools conveniently spaced for secluded swimming.

Miners Bridge is soon passed to your R, and after this the path swings more westwards away from the rushing torrents of the

2M:4 An attractive view of Slater Bridge, Little Langdale

2M:5 Wetherlam reflected in the cold, clear waters of the river Brathay

beck. Further on, another route from the Walna Scar road comes in from the s in the vicinity of Crowberry Haws. Along here, as further height is gained, the magnificent and when dark clouds are scurrying menacingly across the sky, somewhat formidable, easterly aspects of the Coniston Fells are revealed with their massive high-level combes, intervening craggy ridges and dominating, bowl-shaped skyline. The slopes of Coniston Old Man, Brim Fell, Little and Great How Crags and Swirl How, and the massive finger-like, southern ridges of Black Sails and Lad Stones snaking to the summit of Wetherlam, are all visible in favourable weather from this general area.

After turning R along the wide track from the Walna Scar road it is important to avoid the next track off to your R, but after passing this, follow the winding, rocky route that climbs the steep, craggy fellside to your R. Next a series of apparently never-ending zigzags, tortuously scale the steeper slopes of the fell passing through former quarry workings to bring you, at last, to the cool, crystal clear, welcoming blue waters of Low Water. There is one further junction in the path before the tarn is reached, and at this, bear R again climbing round the R outside flank of the fell. The tiny tarn is concealed within the embrace of the folded fell until almost the last moment. This is a good spot to linger, as it is the only stretch of inviting water visited during the entire stage.

From the tarn a rocky, and then quite badly eroded stony, compressed gravel and clay path winds relentlessly sw up the final steep slopes of the fell to the summit of Coniston Old Man, to join up with the main route.

The way to Swirl How   *(Allow 1½ hours)*

From the top of Coniston Old Man use the directions given in the main route to reach the summit of Swirl How, some 3 km (1¾ miles) away to the N along a pleasant, undulating high-level ridge route.

2E:1 Low Water, Levers Water and Wetherlam

The way to Elterwater   *(Allow 3 hours)*

Leave the summit of Swirl How along the pathway to the w. The route then bends progressively to the N following the Top of Broad Slack along a clear, cairned path, to reach Great Carrs. The remains of the crashed aircraft may be visited to your L near here; this poignant spot is marked by a simple cross. From Great Carrs there is an obvious descent along the attractively broad ridge of Greenburn to the NE by way of Little Carrs, Hell Gill Pike, Wet Side Edge and High End. There is some easy scrambling involved on the way down, but be particularly careful of the dangerous edge to your R.

There are several alternative paths to choose from on the way down, but endeavour to keep towards the crest of the ridge and veer further to your R as the craggy fellside surrenders to easier, grassy slopes. Then there is one final craggy section that you descend ESE, once more veering to your R and in this process passing a solitary holly tree. (There are alternative descent paths either side of this landmark.) Select the R-hand path at the bottom of the final craggy section, and the way from here leads down to Greenburn Beck across some open fellside that at times can be severely waterlogged.

The stream is crossed to the E of Greenburn reservoir, near MR 292022, and the continuing, lower path to your L soon joins up with the main route, descending on your R a little further down the valley. From here follow the directions provided in the main route to reach Elterwater village about 4 km (2½ miles) away to the NE.

FURTHER CURTAILMENT

There are several possibilities of reaching Little Langdale Valley from Coniston without having to scale Coniston Old Man. In terms of decreasing severity these range from (*1*) walking NW from Coniston, first up the Coppermines Valley and then along the E shore of Levers Water to reach Swirl Hawse, where either Prison Band to the WSW can be scaled to join the easier route prescribed above, or from Swirl Hawse by climbing NE the remainder of the main route over Wetherlam may be followed, to (*2*) walking along the pleasant pass over Hole Rake to reach the car parking area at Tilberthwaite to the E of Wetherlam and then using the track leading N from High Tilberthwaite to arrive at the merged main and easier routes just to the s of Little Langdale Tarn.

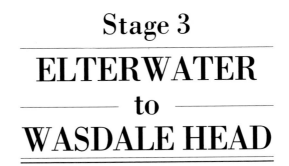

Stage 3

ELTERWATER
to
WASDALE HEAD

Photograph: The route westwards over
Bow Fell

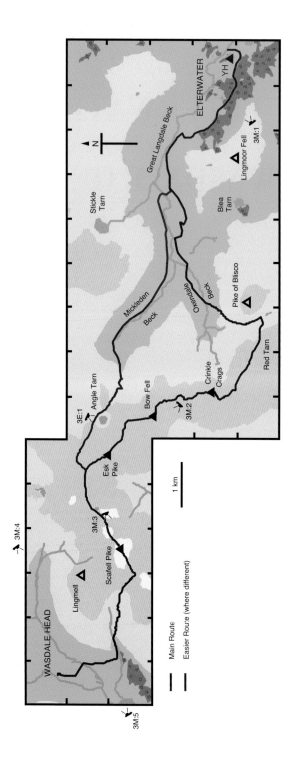

**STAGE 3
ELTERWATER TO
WASDALE HEAD**

ELTERWATER

YH

Lingmoor Fell

3M:1

Great Langdale Beck

N

Stickle
Tarn

Blea
Tarn

Pike of Blisco

Mickleden

Oxendale

Beck

Beck

Red Tarn

Angle Tarn

Bow Fell

Crinkle
Crags

3E:1

3M:2

Esk
Pike

1 km

3M:4

3M:3

Scafell Pike

Lingmell

Main Route

Easier Route (where different)

WASDALE HEAD

3M:5

TIME ALLOWANCE
Main Route: 9 hours
Easier Route: 7½ hours

STARTING LOCATION

Elterwater village, just off the B5343 road in Great Langdale Valley, about 5½ km (3½ miles) w of Ambleside.
OLM6/MR 328048.
Two car parks in village – hold about 50 cars in total.
Start walk from village green.

OVERVIEW/INTEREST

Highlight of this stage is Scafell Pike 978 m (3210 ft), the highest place in England.
Route leads into the craggy, volcanic heartland of the Lakeland Fells.
Main route takes in Crinkle Crags and Bow Fell.
High-level landscape is unique: mountain massifs contrasting with the warm, green tranquil valleys below, in which the major lakes radiate.
One of the great walks of the Lake District.

FOOTPATHS

Very adequate, and not too severely eroded: worst stretch is approaching the top of Rossett Gill on the easier route.
(Some good renovations of parts of the two routes have been carried out: on the main route climbing out of Oxendale and on the lower section of Rossett Gill at the end of Mickleden on the easier route.)
The way is clear, marked with numerous cairns and there are no significant wet areas.
The way over Crinkle Crags and across Bow Fell and Esk Pike demands care in misty conditions.

Statistics	Main route		Easier route	
	Km	**Miles**	**Km**	**Miles**
Distance walked	23.0	14.3	19.2	11.9
	M	**Feet**	**M**	**Feet**
Height climbed	1540	5050	1120	3670
Principal Peaks	**M**	**Feet**	**M**	**Feet**
Crinkle Crags	859	2816	—	—
Bow Fell	902	2960	—	—
Esk Pike	885	2903	—	—
Scafell Pike	978	3210	978	3210

Stage 3 Elterwater to Wasdale Head

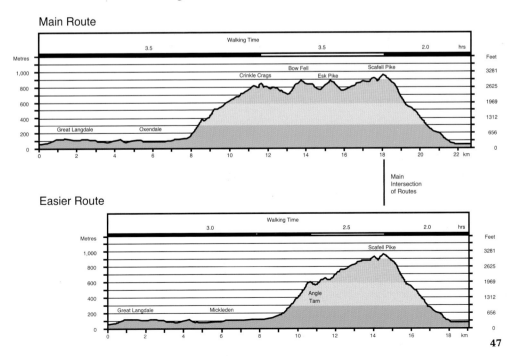

MAIN ROUTE   *(Allow 9 hours)*

The way to Crinkle Crags   *(Allow 3½ hours)*

From the village green select the minor road to the s signed to Coniston and Little Langdale. At the Eltermere Country House Hotel turn up the lane on your R and keep R along the surfaced way, avoiding first the footpath uphill on your L to Little Langdale, then a bridleway on your L that leads to Lingmoor Fell, followed by another on your R that descends to Chapel Stile. Past Crossgates Cottage the way penetrates a deciduous forest containing beech, ash, oak and sycamore.

On emerging from this canopy there is a fine unrestricted view ahead and to your R of the flat, neatly farmed Great Langdale Valley flanked by Blea Rigg and the Langdale Pikes to the N and by Lingmoor Fell to the s. Pass Baysbrown Farm and continue along the clearly marked bridleway WNW to Oak Howe cottage following the helpful blue arrowhead markers, as the way degenerates into a rough, rocky track. Continue westwards along the footpath from here towards the head of the valley, as the guiding arrowheads change their colour to yellow.

The path then hugs the lower slopes of Lingmoor Fell, rising steeply on your L as Oak Howe Needle, before it descends to Side House Farm. Exciting views open up hereabouts of Bow Fell, Crinkle Crags, Pike of Blisco and Side Pike. Do not cross the beck but continue w, skirting above the farm buildings. A less distinct path leads you further up the valley and on approaching the large camp site veer R downhill to gain entry to this at a stile followed by a K-gate. Turn L and walk through the site to its westerly end where a further stile at a gap in the stone wall provides access to the valley road.

Turn R and, when the road bends sharp R, select the footpath on your L that leads to Oxendale and The Band via Stool End Farm. Beyond the farm continue w up into Oxendale avoiding a branch path on your R that climbs The Band. Cross the splendid footbridge over Oxendale Beck dedicated to two young mountain climbers, and continue along the obvious rocky, steep path round Brown Howe to gain the col above Browney Gill. The reconstruction work carried out along here in the form of stepped terracing has been superbly executed.

The next part of the route is through a high-level combe beside the deep gully of Browney Gill and then, near the top of

3M:1 The tiny hamlet of Chapel Stile dwarfed by Helvellyn and Fairfield

the hause, take the L fork, cross the main path between Pike of Blisco and Crinkle Crags and continue the short distance SSE down to Red Tarn. This is well worth the short detour and a pleasant place to take some refreshment.

Retrace your steps to the main path and turn L along it as it sweeps up the fell westwards round the crag of Great Knott. The coast can be seen from here on a fine day, as too can the peak of Dow Crag prominent amongst the Coniston Fells. Your path approaches the first of The Crinkles surprisingly from a westerly direction, before meandering northwards through a bewildering array of craggy buffs and intervening cols of shattered rock. These probably result from long spent glacial action followed by severe frost fracturing.

Soon the pronounced gully that houses 'Bad Step' is reached and the accepted scramble is up the easy rock face on the R of the fault-line where there are convenient foot and hand holds. Unless you are an experienced rock climber on no account be tempted to climb straight up the gully because there is a difficult overhang there, and on one occasion we came across a walker trapped fast in this by his unwieldy rucksack and who needed assistance to be released. A less adventurous ascent round the Step is by the path to the L, but if you choose this way be careful to head E at the top to relocate immediately the main path northwards. This and the next section are particularly difficult to negotiate in mist and low cloud and therefore, in this vicinity, continuouly check your direction of travel by taking frequent compass bearings! As the name suggests there are several summit crags on The Crinkles and the most interesting sights on these are probably the impressive rock formations and the steep fall-aways into upper Oxendale far below you to the E. These sights, especially in the ever-changing light patterns of inclement weather, are fascinatingly foreboding.

The way to Scafell Pike   *(Allow 3½ hours)*

Descend from Crinkle Crags along the highest ridge path that leads between N and NNW, and do not deviate down any of the tempting ways to your L as these will inevitably lead you astray towards Lingcove Beck. The final descent to your next certain landmark of The Three Tarns, a main feature situated at MR 248060, is along a rocky zigzag path that drops steeply NNW to the hause below.

Past the tarns, a cairned path gains height equally steeply as it winds through a shallow gully of shattered rock. The way fans out into several alternative routes, through a vast labyrinth of

3M:2 The distinctive profile of the Scafells observed from Three Tarns

boulders that form the extensive summit pinnacle area of Bow Fell, above to the N. The final climb to the top requires some easy scrambling. In clear weather the panorama from this superb viewing platform is simply magnificent and is best viewed in either early morning or late evening sunlight. The array of peaks visible from here include the Langdale Pikes, Side Pike and Lingmoor Fell, Pike of Blisco, Wetherlam, the Coniston Fells, Crinkle Crags, Harter Fell, Muster Fell, the Scafell group, Pillar, Great End, the Gables, Esk Pike, Grasmoor, Crag Hill, Grisedale Pike, Glaramara, Skiddaw, Blencathra, Helvellyn and Fairfield.

Leave Bow Fell by continuing to walk NNW in the direction of Esk Pike, and in misty weather check your compass bearing frequently because the terrain hereabouts contains rocks and minerals that are magnetic and therefore individual compass readings should be viewed circumspectly. Initially the path twists down steeply through boulders, but then the way progressively flattens off along a clearly cairn-marked path as it veers westwards to reach the hause of Ore Gap.

Another steepish climb follows, this time NW to reach the summit of Esk Pike where several horizons have to be gained before the top is eventually reached. This is an equally craggy, but quite different, summit to that of Bow Fell. A further descent follows, still walking NW, to pass to the W of the level ground of Esk Hause, a famous meeting point of several mountain routes.

Your way continues westwards up to the shallow col that links Great End to the rest of the Scafell ridge. Morecambe Bay is visible from here on a clear day. Veer L along the main ridge, using the well-trodden, cairned way over the worn rock formations. Your direction is now wsw. The obvious path bisects Broad Crag and Ill Crag prior to your descent over large boulders and then a steep scree slope to the narrow col separating Piers Gill and Little Narrowcove. Then one final thrust up the steepish, rocky slope ahead to reach the summit of Scafell Pike, standing at 978 m (3210 ft), the highest elevation in England. Additional to the extensive panorama previously revealed from the top of Bow Fell, good views of the following additional mountain scenery may be observed in good weather from the extensive summit area of this lofty fell: Sca Fell, Wast Water, Yewbarrow, Mosedale Horseshoe, Kirk Fell, High Stile group, Grisedale Pike, Robinson, Hindscarth and Dale Head, Sty Head Tarn, Maiden Moor, Borrowdale and Derwent Water, Eskdale and the far off coastline. If you are extremely fortunate it is possible to see Snowdon in exceptionally clear weather. I have seen it once from here and I have been told that one of the National Park rangers who visits the spot more regularly has seen it twice in forty years! Who knows, you may be lucky!

3M:3 Striding out towards the summit of Scafell Pike

3M:4 Wasdale exposed from the commanding summit of Great Gable

The way to Wasdale Head   *(Allow 2 hours)*

Leave the summit area of Scafell Pike by descending along the cairned path to the sw in the direction of Sca Fell. This path threads down a rough, rock strewn slope to the hause of Mickledore. Here the challenging climbs and scrambles up the rock faces of Sca Fell lie further ahead to the sw, but on this occasion your route avoids these by bearing away nw, to descend down the cairned path to the s of Hollow Stones, across Lingmell Gill and then finally takes you northwards towards Wasdale Head.

The wider Lingmell Beck is crossed, after which the path veers westwards to reach the valley road about ½ km (⅓ mile) to the s of the hamlet of Wasdale Head. Overnight accommodation at the head of the valley is very limited and depending upon where you intend to stay, perhaps at one of the outlying farms, you may wish to trim your final approach route to head directly to some pre-booked location.

[AUTHOR'S NOTE: The National Park rangers believe this suggested main route is too long and difficult in bad weather, and therefore in these conditions you are strongly advised to select one of the easier alternatives.]

EXTENSIONS FOR EXTREMELY STRONG WALKERS

The route is a long and challenging one and as there is plenty to interest you on the way, time passes very quickly indeed, so be careful in choosing any additional objectives. See also cautionary note above!

Amongst those extensions to be considered is a more thorough exploration of the main Scafell ridge, and the separate rocky summits of Great End, Broad Crag and Ill Crag are all well worth a visit for the additional vantage points provided. The longer and more demanding final descent from Scafell Pike by way of Lingmell is also worth contemplating.

Exceptionally fit and fast walkers may, however, think about adding an extra dimension to the start of this stage by either climbing up Pike of Blisco from the head of the Langdale Valley, or undertaking an even more formidable challenge by first using the high-level route of Lingmoor Fell and then traversing round Side Pike to reach the high ground above the Langdale Valley as a preliminary to then continuing by way of Pike of Blisco. If you do decide on this final mammoth undertaking, be careful when traversing round Side Pike to pass, at one point, between the rocky buttresses of the mountain and an outlying finger of rock. Do not be tempted to descend from the path through this gap and go round the outside of the needle of rock as this is relatively dangerous.

3M:5 Looking across Wast Water towards Great Gable and Scafell Pike

EASIER ROUTE   *(Allow 7½ hours)*

The way to the top of Rossett Gill   *(Allow 3 hours)*

Follow the directions given for the main route up Great Langdale Valley as far as Side House Farm, situated at MR 295060. Turn R here, cross the small beck, and then use the path and bridge over Great Langdale Beck to reach the valley road beyond. Cross this and proceed westwards along the N side of the valley along the footpaths that will guide you round The Old Dungeon Ghyll Hotel and Middle Fell Farm into Mickleden.

The route along the flat ground of Mickleden, beside Mickleden Beck is part of The Cumbria Way and the path is uneventfully straightforward. The valley is, however, wild and remote and the area is botanically noted for its profusion of *Digitalis* (foxglove). The broad path leads NW to Rossett Gill and Stake Pass, as ahead the craggy skyline becomes progressively dominated by Bow Fell and Rossett Pike. Cross the beck by the wooden bridge at the head of the valley, and fork L up the path signed to Esk Hause that climbs up by the side of Rossett Gill.

Extensive restoration work, quite superbly undertaken, has arrested the severe erosion on the lower sections of the route through this fault-line. There are two distinct ways up to the top of the pass, either straight up the unstable steep-sided gully or a newer path off to the L which traverses upwards along a more comfortable gradient. There are also mini-alternatives along many sections of each of these. Both ways converge near the top, close to a massive cairn that inconveniently straddles the wide eroded path here. A short distance further on the tranquil and remote Angle Tarn comes into view below, wrapped within the steep, precipitous NE slopes of Bow Fell and Esk Pike.

The way to Scafell Pike   *(Allow 2½ hours)*

Walk down to and past Angle Tarn, and then climb the steep eroded path exiting from the combe and leading NW. The broad path winds up to the shelter near Esk Hause in the form of an impressive stone cross. Continue uphill, passing the shelter to your R, along a broad, eroded path. When this path divides either choice will lead you towards the col between Great End and the rest of the Scafell ridge. After a short distance another path converges from the L; this is the way down from Esk Pike and you join the main route at this point (MR 233081). Continue along the main route to reach the summit of Scafell Pike about 2 km (1¼ miles) away to the SW.

The way to Wasdale Head   *(Allow 2 hours)*

Follow the directions given for the main route to descend to Wasdale Head.

FURTHER CURTAILMENT

The easier route described above is based upon the belief that you will wish to stand on the summit of the highest mountain in England. If this is not the case and you wish to follow a shorter and less demanding way still, the obvious alternative is, from the vicinity of the shelter near Esk Hause (MR 235082), to simply descend along the well-defined path to the NW that winds round Great End and past Sprinkling Tarn down to Sty Head. From here another obvious path leads down, with some easy scrambling involved, over Toad How and Bursting Knott to Wasdale Head below, following the course of Lingmell Beck in a westward direction.

3E:1 Approaching Angle Tarn nestling below Esk Pike and Bow Fell

Stage 4

WASDALE HEAD
to
BUTTERMERE

Photograph: Wasdale Head and the
entrance to Mosedale

STAGE 4 WASDALE HEAD TO BUTTERMERE

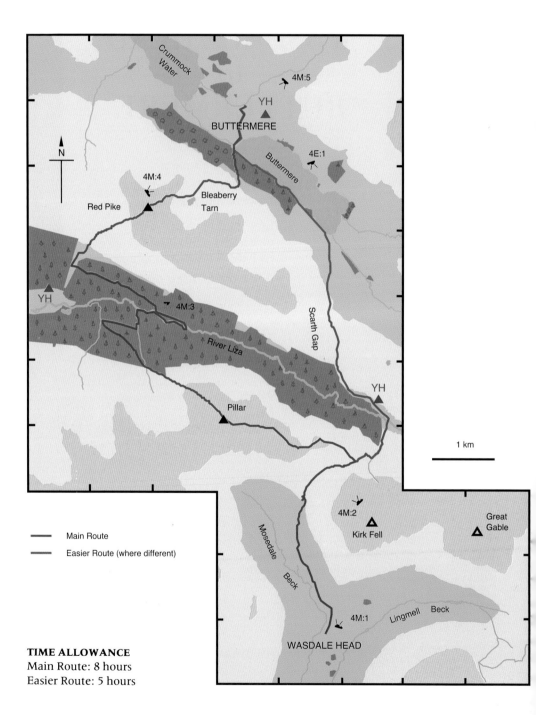

TIME ALLOWANCE
Main Route: 8 hours
Easier Route: 5 hours

STARTING LOCATION

Wasdale Head, tiny hamlet 15 km (9¼ miles) NE of the village of Gosforth, which lies just off the A595 (T) road.
OLM 6/MR 187088.
Substantial parking around village green.
Start walk from the Wasdale Head Inn.

OVERVIEW/INTEREST

Route passes over two formidable mountain chains, the Pillar and High Stile fells.
Between these is steep-sided Ennerdale valley, with dense stretches of conifers, and through which flows the River Liza.
One of the finest and most satisfying high-level walks in the whole of Lakeland.

FOOTPATHS

With two exceptions footpaths are good and route finding presents few difficulties.
The problems are (1) there is no entirely satisfactory route down from Pillar that links conveniently and easily with the subsequent ascent of Red Pike, and (2) the final long, tiring descent from Red Pike is initially down badly eroded, steep slopes followed by having to walk down the most awkward, man-made, stony terracing!
Wet patches and boggy sections virtually non-existent, save for one stretch through Ennerdale forest.

Statistics	Main route		Easier route	
	Km	**Miles**	**Km**	**Miles**
Distance walked	17.8	11.1	11.1	6.9
	M	**Feet**	**M**	**Feet**
Height climbed	1500	4920	670	2200
Principal Peaks	**M**	**Feet**	**M**	**Feet**
Pillar	892	2927	—	—
Red Pike (Buttermere)	755	2479	—	—

Stage 4 Wasdale Head to Buttermere

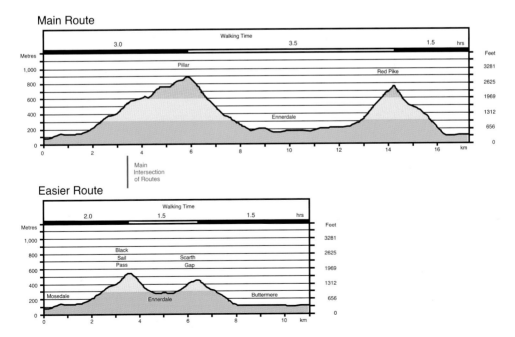

MAIN ROUTE   *(Allow 8 hours)*

The way to Pillar   *(Allow 3 hours)*

From the side of the Inn choose the bridleway which keeps to the R of Mosedale Beck and is signed to Black Sail Pass. The first part of the walk is northwards, climbing initially quite gradually into Mosedale beside the beck. The gradient gradually steepens as progress is made towards the top of the pass where the slopes sweep upwards into the craggy, high peaks far above. The path is exceptionally straightforward to follow and you can therefore concentrate on admiring the splendid array of mountains, including the formidable Mosedale Horseshoe. Although all their summits are not visible until you attain greater height, these fells include Kirk Fell, Looking Stead, Pillar, Little Scoat Fell, Red Pike and Yewbarrow. There are also the infamous, now worn down, Dorehead Screes, precipitously falling from the western flank of this lofty encirclement.

4M:1 A tranquil view of Mosedale Beck early in the morning

4M:2 Pillar spotted from the crags of Kirk Fell

At the top of Black Sail Pass turn L and walk up the path heading WNW. The route then progressively gains higher ground in a delightful variety of ascent sections, some gentle, others steeper and more demanding up rocky paths with some easy scrambling. There are intervening, long-sweeping, rounded slopes, along a way that is well cairned. During this part of the climb there are many views to be appreciated on a clear day, including a glimpse of the Irish Sea, Wast Water and Burnmoor Tarn, whilst amongst the fells coming into view are the far distant craggy pinnacles of the Scafells, and the rounded outline of Skiddaw. Dominating the landscape ahead, WNW, is the higher ground separating you from the summit of Pillar.

During your ascent of Pillar you will pass a series of deep gullies and chasms, close-to-foot on your R-hand side, and these are worth observing as you pass by from the safety of the broad top ridge. At last the ground levels off into the vast, unexpectedly flat summit area of Pillar with its features of a shelter, a trigonometric point and an impressive cairn. In favourable weather the following outstanding scenery can be observed: Scafell group and Harter Fell, Illgill Head and Whin Rigg Ridge, Wasdale Red Pike and Haycock, Scoat Fell and Steeple, Ennerdale Water, Crummock Water, Buttermere Red Pike and Grasmoor, Skiddaw beyond Causey Pike and Robinson, Blencathra, Helvellyn group, Glaramara, Great Gable and Bow Fell.

The way to Red Pike (Buttermere)   *(Allow 3¹/₂ hours)*

Descend NW from the summit area passing a small shelter to your R, and immediately locate and follow a cairned path leading down towards the head of Ennerdale Water. Precipitous slopes lurk further to your R so be particularly vigilant here in misty conditions. When the lower slopes come into view take a compass bearing on the location where the stream High Beck enters the forested area and resolutely keep to this line of travel. It is NW. The long descent, first over steep, rocky sections and then down progressively lessening rates of fall as grassy slopes are penetrated, will eventually bring you to the boundary of the forested area at High Beck.

Cross High Beck before entering the forest, and therefore ignore the first seductive stile and an inviting grassy pathway leading down from there into the trees as this soon peters out in difficult, steeply wooded terrain. Safely across the fast-flowing beck, continue eastwards for a short distance along a faint path beside the forest fence and then cross the fence at the next stile provided. A better defined path will now lead you downwards, soon on a NNW diagonal, to a forestry road. Cross this on your approach diagonal and continue to descend along the path on the far side, the start of which is indicated by a cairn.

When last visited the next section was quite exacting, due in part to considerable debris abandoned after tree harvesting operations and in part to the waterlogged rutted slope. (The forestry rangers have been informed of this and, within their finite resources, I am confident they will carry out remedial work on this section of the path as quickly as possible.) Beyond a stile adjacent to a post, bearing at the time, an orange marker circle, is a continuation path which leads to the Forestry Commission's 'Nine Becks Walk' along Ennerdale. Turn R here and use the next section of this narrow, but well-established path, marked with posts carrying blue circles, to walk E along the valley.

At a line of mature conifers the trail turns sharply L, downhill, and after using the bridge at the forestry road below, to cross the stream on your R, turn immediately L again down the continuation of the trail. This leads to the River Liza cutting its course deep into the valley floor below. Turn R along the river bank and follow the gushing waters upstream to reach a wide forest road where you cross the Liza by the substantial bridge.

4M:3 Steeple and Black Crag observed from Ennerdale

4M:4 The north-westerly fells seen in late evening sunshine from the top of Red Pike

Now turn L, and walk back WNW down the main valley road through the forest. After about ½ km (⅓ mile) turn R along the path signed 'Nine Becks Walk' and within a short distance veer R again up an attractive minor forest road that immediately bends L. This lane then levels off, and just before it commences to descend, locate an important marker on your R that indicates a path, the continuation of the Nine Becks Walk, that you now need to follow. This is at MR 152144. Last time visited, there was a very indistinct exit route from the road and the subsequent path through the trees only becomes intermittently well established as it leads diagonally upwards to the NW. (Again the forest rangers have been alerted.) After crossing a stream by a footbridge the edge of the trees is soon reached, beyond which a short stretch of open fellside has to be crossed to connect with the clearly established path to the top of Red Pike coming up from High Gillerthwaite.

Now veer R, up the broad, steepish slope and access the open fellside at the gate and stile ahead. A long and severe climb now challenges you as you trudge up the relentlessly rising slopes. The way ascends to a shallow col to the NE that links Little Dodd to Red Pike. Then quite suddenly you are there standing on the summit of Red Pike. This will almost certainly be towards evening when the breathtaking variety of views to be observed

in favourable weather-conditions in soft, waning, sunlight are at their best.

New sightings from this summit include The Dodds and Great Borne; Hen Comb with Blake Fell and Carling Knott further behind; Loweswater and Mellbreak, Crummock Water, Grasmoor; Whiteless Pike with Crag Hill and Sail in the background; Causey Pike in front of Skiddaw and Blencathra silhouetted on the distant horizon; Robinson, Hindscarth and Dale Head, Fleetwith Pike and High Stile. A fitting recompense for the exhausting climb up.

[AUTHOR'S NOTE: The National Park rangers have suggested an alternative route from the summit of Pillar to reach Red Pike. Their recommendation is to first return to Black Sail Pass, and from there to descend into upper Ennerdale. This is followed by climbing up Scarth Gap, before scrambling onto the summit of High Crag. From High Crag the ridge westwards over High Stile is followed, to re-connect with the suggested main route at the summit of Red Pike.

Should you decide to use this recommended alternative route, beware that the paths leading up the steep slopes from Scarth Gap are composed of compressed earth and footholds in icy conditions are difficult to maintain, so exercise great care.]

The way to Buttermere Village   *(Allow 1½ hours)*

Descend from Red Pike to the ENE along the wide way marked by cairns. The very steep, dangerously eroded path twists and turns several times before the easier, flatter ground at Bleaberry Tarn is thankfully attained. Be particularly careful making your way down these demanding upper slopes. Pass the tarn with it on your R. Next cross the exit stream from the tarn that soon falls dramatically as Sourmilk Gill. A stony path ENE leads to a long traverse that somewhat disconcertingly insists, for some distance, in leading you away from a direct descent towards Buttermere village.

This is followed by having to negotiate a series of steep zigzags along a renovated part of the pathway, the make-up of which is irritatingly wrongly angled and agonising to descend with tired and aching leg muscles and painful toes at the end of a long day on the fells. Beyond a gate, a final, long traverse down through mixed woodlands leads to the comfortable lower pathways that will guide you into Buttermere village. At this stage, it is reassuring to know that it is less than 1 km (⅔ mile) away across absolutely flat land to the N.

4M:5 High Stile and Red Pike, Buttermere revealed from near Mill Beck

EXTENSIONS FOR STRONG WALKERS

This stage of the route involves a long, strenuous day on the fells with two steep climbs, and no extensions are advocated to the route described, even for strong walkers, other than minor additional explorations along the way such as, perhaps, descending from Red Pike by way of The Saddle.

For those who must, the climb out of Wasdale could be undertaken via Kirk Fell or even one of the routes up Great Gable and then Kirk Fell before descending to join the main route described at the top of Black Sail Pass. However, these suggestions are strictly for those few with the appetite for devouring rough mountain terrain and with the stamina of fell runners. No other persons should attempt these extreme extensions!

4E:1 Hay Stacks and Buttermere captured in early morning sunshine

EASIER ROUTE   *(Allow 5 hours)*

The way to Black Sail Pass   *(Allow 2 hours)*

Follow the directions given in the main route to reach the top of Black Sail Pass at MR 192115.

The way to Scarth Gap   *(Allow 1½ hours)*

From Black Sail Pass there is an obvious descent along a well-established path down into upper Ennerdale. There are a few rocky, steepish sections but otherwise the way down is very straightforward and the descent can be quite quickly accomplished. Cross the infant River Liza by the footbridge provided, and on which it is worth pausing to catch your breath and to take time to appreciate the contrasting views which can be enjoyed up and down stream.

The path rises from river level and the strategically positioned Black Sail Hut YH is soon passed on your R. From here the path continues to gain height at an increasing rate beside the line of the forested area on your L as it climbs with great certainty to the top of Scarth Gap. This lies in quite formidable wild and boulder strewn terrain between craggy Hay Stacks to the E and the equally steep and rocky slopes of High Crag to the NW.

The way to Buttermere Village   *(Allow 1½ hours)*

There is a pleasant, but a longer and a slightly more adventurous descent from Scarth Gap into Buttermere than from Black Sail pass into upper Ennerdale. Most of the way is down an exacting rocky, stony or gravel path and there are some steep sections where sometimes you have to compete with a water course for foot space. The final diagonal traverse to the SW tip of Buttermere Lake is less demanding as inviting views appear of the pretty valley and wooded lake shores below.

The continuation path to the NW through Burtness Wood beside the lake is delightful. Keep to the lower route here as it is the more attractive one, providing better, less restricted views across the water, particularly so in the direction of the village and of Whiteless Pike and Grasmoor towering above. Buttermere Dubbs are crossed at the footbridge, after which there are obvious footpaths and farm lanes to lead you into the village to the N.

FURTHER CURTAILMENT

Just as the main route was a particularly strenuous stage, the easier route between Wasdale Head and Buttermere village is exceptionally effortless. It is also straightforward and navigation presents few, if any problems. For these reasons, no further curtailment is suggested. (In any case it would be difficult to propose any further practicable curtailment.)

Stage 5

BUTTERMERE
to
BRAITHWAITE

Photograph: The climb to Whiteless
Pike provides fine views of Rannerdale
Knotts and Mellbreak

STAGE 5 BUTTERMERE TO BRAITHWAITE

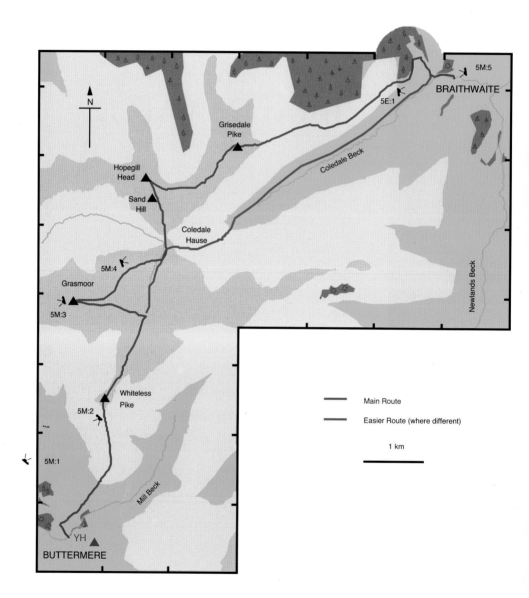

5M:5

BRAITHWAITE

5E:1

Grisedale
Pike

Coledale Beck

Hopegill
Head

Sand
Hill

Coledale
Hause

N

Newlands Beck

5M:4

Grasmoor

5M:3

Whiteless
Pike

5M:2

5M:1

Mill Beck

YH

BUTTERMERE

—— Main Route

—— Easier Route (where different)

1 km

TIME ALLOWANCE
Main Route: 6½ hours
Easier Route: 5 hours

STARTING LOCATION

Buttermere village, at the N end of Buttermere Lake, on the B5289 road.

OLM 4/MR 175169.

Parking in and above village – room for over 70 cars.

Start walk on the B5289 road heading W.

OVERVIEW/INTEREST

A walk dominated by the bulk of Grasmoor, a high mountain with a large, flattish summit area.

Soft, grassy slopes of the Skiddaw Slates provide a pleasant contrast to the harsh landscape of the central fells.

Route includes Whiteless Pike and Grisedale Pike: excellent views from both peaks.

Lakes of Buttermere, Crummock Water, Loweswater, Derwent Water and Bassenthwaite are all visible along the route on a clear day.

FOOTPATHS

The footpaths are extremely good and the route is straightforward. There is some erosion in places but this presents few problems. Coming off Grisedale Pike is probably the most demanding stretch.

Statistics	Main route		Easier route	
	Km	**Miles**	**Km**	**Miles**
Distance walked	13.8	8.6	10.3	6.4
	M	**Feet**	**M**	**Feet**
Height climbed	1100	3610	670	2200
Principal Peaks	**M**	**Feet**	**M**	**Feet**
Whiteless Pike	660	2159	660	2159
Grasmoor	852	2791	—	—
Hopegill Head	770	2525	—	—
Grisedale Pike	791	2593	—	—

Stage 5 Buttermere to Braithwaite

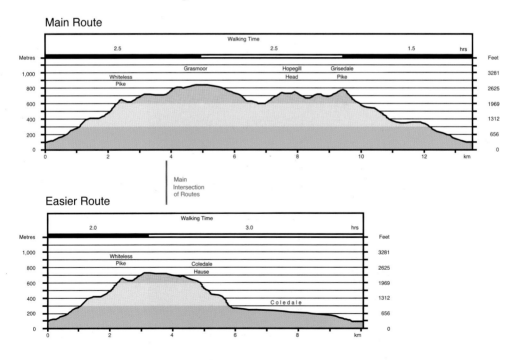

MAIN ROUTE   *(Allow 6½ hours)*

The way to Grasmoor   *(Allow 2½ hours)*

Leave the village by the B5289 road, passing the Bridge Hotel and heading w towards Crummock Water. Walk uphilll, and opposite Crag Farm select the grassy footpath on the R that leads up the fellside, initially back on an acute angle to the L of some dwellings. The direction is now NE. Soon the path divides into three ways; continue up the middle one that can be seen snaking up the fellside towards Whiteless Breast above. You are now treading along a pleasant path leading upwards through bracken, and soon your route will veer to the L in line with a craggy outcrop above. At the next division in the path, take the one on the R heading NNE. This leads to a prominent cairn that marks the top of Rannerdale. The views from this area are superb, both down over Buttermere and beyond to the impressive fells of the High Stile ridge, and westwards down Rannerdale towards Crummock Water.

The next stretch is along the narrow, stony path to your L, heading N. This zigzags up the steeper, craggier fellside to reach Whiteless Breast. (There is a traverse to the L round this knoll).

5M:1 Crummock Water, Rannerdale and Whiteless Pike viewed from Mellbreak

5M:2 Looking down Rannerdale towards Crummock Water and Loweswater

From here a narrow but well-established path winds to the top of Whiteless Pike up a progressively steepening gradient. Again the direct path bypasses the summit and to reach the cairn there, make the short diversion up the fellside to your L. Then walk along Whiteless Edge, before the path continues NNE across the flatter ground of Wandope Moss to deposit you at the col between Crag Hill and Grasmoor.

Veer L along the obvious side path, as a prelude to climbing the higher slopes of the Grasmoor massif away to the w. A steepish incline follows before the ground once again levels off as the wide, gravel path snakes round the upper fellside to bring you to the broad, flat summit area to your R. The path leads directly to a large, welcoming stone shelter. There is a plethora of viewing positions lining this expansive summit area, and all of these are worth your inspection. In exceptionally clear weather the Isle of Man and Scotland are visible from here, and nearer to, in addition to the features already positioned, the splendid ridge of Gasgale Crags are quite spectacular when viewed from the northern rim of the Grasmoor summit.

The way to Grisedale Pike   *(Allow 2½ hours)*

In bad weather retrace your final approach steps down to the hause separating Grasmoor from Crag Hill, but towards the bottom veer L to rendezvous with the path below, at MR 187206. From here turn L and follow the well-used route downhill to reach Coledale Hause. In good weather there is a more ambitious way down. This is by walking further to the N along the summit edge of Grasmoor, and descending to the NE to reach the path down to Coledale Hause further to the N than the better-established descent to this pathway previously described. In following this more exciting descent route be careful, as the N edge of Grasmoor in the vicinity of Dove Crags is precipitously steep, and the path here is intermittent with some rough ground to cross before you reach the secure path below leading to Coledale Hause. The rewards for this excursion are the stupendous views into the wild, dark and foreboding recesses of the gouged out combes and shattered rock formations, which form the northerly face of Grasmoor.

At Coledale Hause veer off to your L across the fellside, where the main path steers off to the R before dropping down into Coledale to the NE. At the bottom of the depression, in an area noted for boggy ground that you will do well to completely avoid, take the L fork in the path that climbs quite steeply up the fell to the NNW. A clear path will then lead you, first to Sand Hill, and from there to Hopegill Head. This peak is situated approximately half way along the fine ridge which connects Whiteside with Grisedale Pike.

From Hopegill Head your route heads initially SE, and then more eastwards, along the ridge of Hobcarton Crag to meet up again with the more direct path up from Coledale Hause to Grisedale Pike. A dilapidated stone wall provides a reassuring directional bearing along here. The path now undulates NE along the rocky spur, and after crossing a pool, cairns guide you to the summit of Grisedale Pike. New views to the N open up from here of the extensive coniferous forests of Thornthwaite, and the dominant peaks in this rolling, lower terrain are those of Lord's Seat and Barf.

The way to Braithwaite   *(Allow 1½ hours)*

Descend from Grisedale Pike by the rocky path that contorts down through the steep, rough, easterly approach slopes of the fell. Your direction here is between E and SE. Following this, the

5M:4 A frosty landscape of Grasmoor, Grisedale Pike, Skiddaw and faraway Blencathra

5M:3 A westerly vista from the summit of Grasmoor

stony path drops to the ENE through a tangle of rocks and boulders to the broad, rounded and partially grassed spur of Sleet How. Along this the rate of descent reduces considerably. Continue down the crest of this ridge with the benefit of more stable ground underfoot.

Still walking ENE, the path eventually divides and you continue down the L-hand fork signed 'Footpath'. (The other way down is now badly eroded and as a consequence has been closed.) After the stile, descend along the diagonal that veers to the L and then bends R along a narrowing track. This leads to a flight of steps down to the tiny car park below. Turn R here, and follow the road from Whinlatter Pass down into the village of Braithwaite, a short distance further on.

EXTENSIONS FOR STRONG WALKERS

The route described is neither particularly long nor strenuous. However, because it mainly follows ridge routes, possibilities for additional challenges are somewhat constrained. One possibility is to spend more time in the vicinity of Hopegill Head, and to venture along the separate ridges leading to Whiteside and towards Ladyside Pike. The walk to the summit of Whiteside above Gasgale Crags is particularly exhilarating on a fine day.

There is a longer and harder route from Grasmoor, and this is further to the S by way of Crag Hill, Sail, Causey Pike and Rowling End, descending into the Newlands Valley near Stoneycroft. From here continue N along the minor road and then use the footpath round the lower NE slopes of Barrow to reach the village, by way of Braithwaite Lodge.

5M:5 A colourful corner of Braithwaite

EASIER ROUTE   *(Allow 5 hours)*

The way to The Hause between Crag Hill and Grasmoor   *(Allow 2 hours)*

Use the directions provided in the main route over Whiteless Pike and Wandope Moss for this section of the route.

The way to Braithwaite   *(Allow 3 hours)*

Continue to follow the directions provided for the main route until Coledale Hause is attained. At MR 189212 leave the main route by keeping to the dominant footpath. This veers off to the R round Eel Crags as it descends rapidly NE into upper Coledale. The way leads through disused mine workings and across mine

5E:1 Looking east down Coledale

tracks situated in more level ground before it drops sharply again, to the s of Force Crag.

The continuation route down then crosses several water courses near Low Force followed by passing s of the old workings of Force Crag Mine. A long, pleasant traverse that hugs the lower slopes of the Sleet How ridge beside Coledale Beck completes the walk towards Braithwaite. Eventually the path leads down to a small car park, with the road from Whinlatter Pass beyond. Turn R and follow the road into the village along the main route.

FURTHER CURTAILMENT

No shorter routes are feasible, and as the easier route described is undemanding once the initial steepish climb out of Buttermere over Whiteless Pike has been achieved, there is little necessity for further curtailment.

Stage 6
BRAITHWAITE
to
PORTINSCALE

Photograph: Looking north from the
Cat Bells ridge towards Skiddaw

STAGE 6 BRAITHWAITE TO PORTINSCALE

TIME ALLOWANCE
Main Route: 9 hours
Easier Route: 7 hours

Main Route

Easier Route (where different)

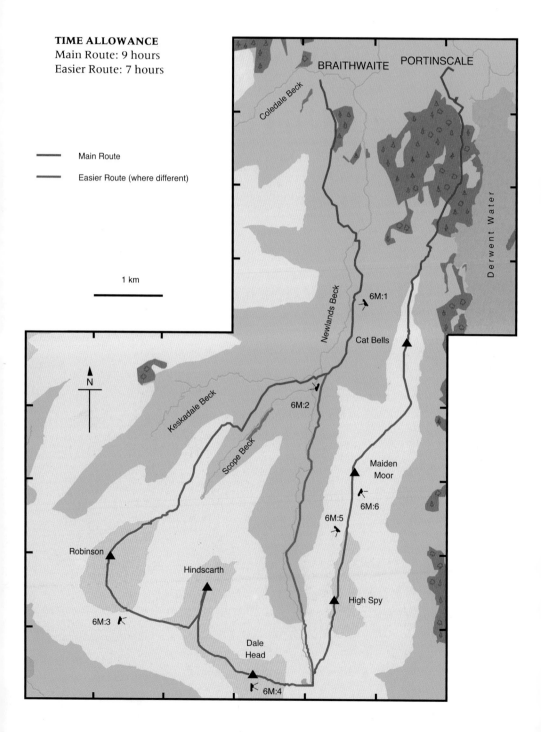

1 km

STARTING LOCATION

Braithwaite village, on the B5292 road, 4 km (2½ miles) w of Keswick.

OLM 4/MR 231236.

Very restricted parking; use area off Whinlatter Pass road – room for fewer than 10 cars.

Start walk from village centre.

OVERVIEW/INTEREST

Flat terrain of Newlands Valley at the beginning contrasts with the subsequent steep slopes of High Snab Bank.

Superb ridge walk follows taking in peaks of Robinson, Hindscarth, Dale Head and High Spy.

Fine views looking down into Borrowdale and across Derwent Water.

Attractive hamlet of Little Town and Newlands Church visited.

FOOTPATHS

Nearly always good and, with two exceptions, route finding is obvious.

Some very easy scrambling is involved on occasions, particularly so on part of the ascent of Robinson over Blea Crags and beyond. The sections of the route that demand particular care are (1) descending from Dale Head to the tarn and (2) during the final approach to Portinscale across the lower ground through Overside Wood. In both there are sections that have several confusing paths and/or intermittent ones.

Statistics	Main route		Easier route	
	Km	**Miles**	**Km**	**Miles**
Distance walked	24.3	15.1	18.8	11.7
	M	**Feet**	**M**	**Feet**
Height climbed	1300	4270	780	2560
Principal Peaks	**M**	**Feet**	**M**	**Feet**
Robinson	737	2417	—	—
Hindscarth	727	2385	—	—
Dale Head	753	2473	—	—
High Spy	653	2143	653	2143
Maiden Moor	576	1887	576	1887

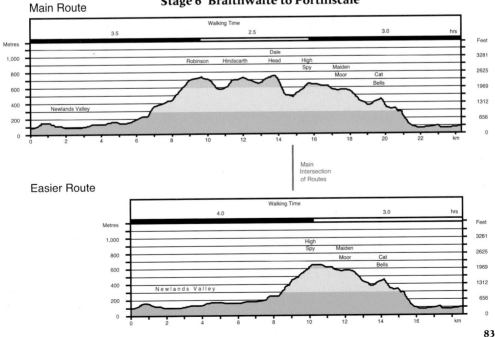

Stage 6 Braithwaite to Portinscale

Main Route

Easier Route

MAIN ROUTE   *(Allow 9 hours)*

The way to Robinson   *(Allow 3½ hours)*

From the village centre take the Newlands Road, heading SE.
After a short distance, at a gate and cattle grid, turn R up the
bridleway to Braithwaite Lodge, skirting this to the R. Continue
uphill over a P-stile and then through a wicket gate at the top of
the next field. Veer immediately L over the brow of the fell
heading towards a tree-fringed skyline. Keep to the lower L-
hand path signed to Newlands. The path runs above a copse of
mixed trees before descending to the Newlands Road.

Use the road for about ½ km (⅓ mile) before turning L down
the footpath to Uzzicar Farm. The farm buildings are passed to
your L, after which a complicated but well-waymarked route
leads through pastures to Newlands Beck, near Stair at MR
236214. Turn L over the bridge and follow the lane round to the
R, passing Newlands Adventure Centre. Continue up the
winding lane southwards to Little Town some 2 km (1¼ miles)
further on. A vista of the high fells you are about to climb opens
up along here. Pass through the hamlet and continue downhill
before turning R over the beck at Chapel Bridge. Take the next
turning on the L to reach Newlands Church.

6M:1 Striding
purposefully up the
Newlands valley

6M:2 Newlands
Church

6M:3 Descending from Robinson towards Hindscarth and Dale Head

Further on, veer L again and walk up the lane passing Low High Snab Cottage and continue beyond the building for about a further ½ km (⅓ mile) before turning R to climb up the steep SE facing side slope of the protruding ridge of High Snab Bank. Follow the less demanding gradient of the crest of this spur SW as it ascends up the rocky features of Blea Crags. These craggy ledges involve some scrambling before the higher ground and the final approach slopes leading to the summit of Robinson are reached. The well worn way up here follows a route that is well marked by cairns, as you keep ascending on a SW diagonal.

The summit area is an interesting mixture of stones, grass and rocky ledges dominated by a large cairn. Prominent peaks visible from here on a good day include Skiddaw, Blencathra, Helvellyn, Hindscarth, Fairfield, Dale Head, Harrison Stickle, Glaramara, Pike of Blisco, Wetherlam, Bow Fell, Esk Pike, the Scafell Massif, Great Gable, Kirk Fell, Hay Stacks, Yewbarrow, the High Stile group, Great Borne, Grasmoor, and Grisedale Pike. A quite superb and revealing mountain panorama. Crummock Water and Loweswater can also be seen in clear weather and the large mountain in between is Mellbreak. (The author has also observed the rare optical phenomenon in this country of 'The Brocken Spectre' and the accompanying 'Glory' on this summit.)

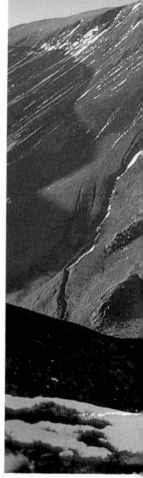

The way to High Spy   *(Allow 2½ hours)*

Depart from Robinson down the gentle slope, along the wide path, walking s. Well-defined ridge paths will then lead you by way of Robinson Crag and Littledale Edge in a sweeping curve across the hause to your L before, after climbing again, you choose the branch path off further to your L, to gain the vast summit area of Hindscarth. This rounded summit is worthy of detailed exploration as the views from here of the route you are traversing are simply stunning, with the mountain features still to come even excelling those already seen.

Depart from Hindscarth to the ssw, retracing for a short distance your final approach steps. Then veer L down the path that further on connects with the direct ridge route between Robinson and Dale Head. Descend to the wide, shallow col below. From here the rocky pinnacles of Hindscarth Edge, climbing se, will lead you to the summit of Dale Head. You are now standing on the highest point of this stage of the walk, and from here many of the most famous mountains in Lakeland are again visible, given favourable weather.

There are several ways down from the summit of Dale Head to the tarn of that name far below. The one favoured is to start by walking s and then follow the good path to your L before veering further L along the route which descends e to pass finally round the s tip of Dalehead Tarn. There are other, more steep ways down, and one of these finishes up by swinging to the N of the tarn. You can encounter difficulties here in misty conditions, and if you lose the path, you may have to traverse down the rough fellside pioneering a unique route of your own. The important point is to keep descending towards the e until you locate the certain landmark of Dalehead Tarn. This is the only significant stretch of water you pass during the entire stage.

Considerable height is surrendered in dropping down to the tarn, and much of it has now to be regained in the subsequent climb to High Spy. The way is now northwards up the steep, craggy slopes of the fell, but there are compensating spectacular views down to your L where the rocky, north-facing buttresses of Dale Head are revealed with the inevitable, steep, scree slopes below plunging down into the valley.

The way to Portinscale   *(Allow 3 hours)*

There is a clear and certain path northwards from High Spy along the ridge. This leads, in succession, over Maiden Moor, down across Hause Gate, up again to the summit of Cat Bells and

6M:5 Hindscarth and Robinson

6M:4 A cairn marks the summit of Dale Head

then one final descent up and over Skelgill Bank before you reach the minor road below near Hawes End. There are delightful open views from this undulating ridge, both down into Borrowdale and across tranquil Derwent Water to Skiddaw and Blencathra. This second view is observed at its best in the dawning light of a frosty winter morning when the rays of the rising sun just start to clip the summits of the fells and render any overnight snow up there a brilliant pink. This is known as the *alpengluh* effect and is due to the early morning light being refracted by its relatively long atmospheric path, this leaving red as the predominant colour.

In the final stages of the descent down the craggy fellside veer R to connect with the road at the junction where a side lane branches off to Skelgill. Walk down the road and across a cattle grid. At the next bend take the footpath off on the R signed 'National Trust – Hawes End'. Cross the surfaced lane to The Hawes End Centre, and proceed through the K-gate opposite, continuing along the footpath directing you towards Portinscale and Keswick.

The next part of the walk is through pleasant open woodlands before Lingholm Gardens are passed. Continue northwards using the footpaths signed to Keswick, Nichol End and Portinscale, crossing two further surfaced drives *en route*. Turn R on reaching the road, and either use this to walk directly into the village or deviate slightly by a more agreeable route. This alternative is achieved by turning L from the road at the next footpath and then a final R turn further along will bring you into the village.

EXTENSIONS FOR STRONG WALKERS

This stage of the route is long and the final undulating, craggy ridge walk from Dalehead Tarn takes a surprisingly long time to complete towards the end of a hard day. Also the way is along all the major spurs in a discrete grouping of high fells and additions, without resorting to further unrealistic descents followed by consequential climbs, are not obvious.

Unsatisfied appetites may be filled by spending more time exploring the interesting side crags along the High Spy/Maiden Moor spur. In particular Minum Crag and the tops of the crags to the w of the main path are well worth a visit. Do be careful though in doing this, as the stunning views of the precipitous rock and scree slopes of Hindscarth are from vantage points along the top of Eel Crags that are also dangerous. On no account attempt to descend to the w down these, not even for a few paces!

EASIER ROUTE   *(Allow 7 hours)*

The way to High Spy   *(Allow 4 hours)*

Use the directions provided in the main route to reach the hamlet of Little Town. From here take the path off to the L that leads southwards along the L bank of the beck, hugging the steep, lower slopes of the Maiden Moor ridge far above. A well-used route climbs progressively ssw up the valley past several disused mine workings, including those of Castlenook. The path bends sse as it scales the upper reaches of the valley, still faithfully following the water course and eventually climbing to pass between the satellite northern crags of Dale Head and Miners Crag before attaining the relatively flat area to the E of Dalehead Tarn. On the way up, the path branches and at this point select the upper L-hand fork that rises more steeply up the rough fellside.

6M:6 Grange-in-Borrowdale with the Dodds in the background

The secluded tarn should be visited as this presents an ideal spot at which to have some refreshments, before you continue your walk northwards to the summit of High Spy. From Dalehead Tarn follow the instructions given in the main route to reach High Spy.

The way to Portinscale *(Allow 3 hours)*

From the summit of High Spy the directions previously given for the main route will lead you to Portinscale.

FURTHER CURTAILMENT

Those walkers who feel they need a rest day only have to walk the short distance of some 2½ km (1½ miles) along the back roads and connecting footpaths to reach Portinscale.

From this extreme, there are many obvious shorter routes other than that described as the easier one, to enjoy a leisurely stroll from Braithwaite to Portinscale, and by consulting the OS Map you should have little difficulty in devising one of your own choosing. One suggestion is to walk to Little Town as described in the main route and then climb eastwards over Hause Gate into Borrowdale. From here the attractive paths round the indented w shore of Derwent Water may be used to reach the National Trust area at Hawes End. This will connect you with the prescribed routes that from here both take an identical way into Portinscale.

Stage 7

PORTINSCALE
to
THRELKELD

Photograph: The view southwards
from the approach slopes of Skiddaw

STAGE 7 PORTINSCALE TO THRELKELD

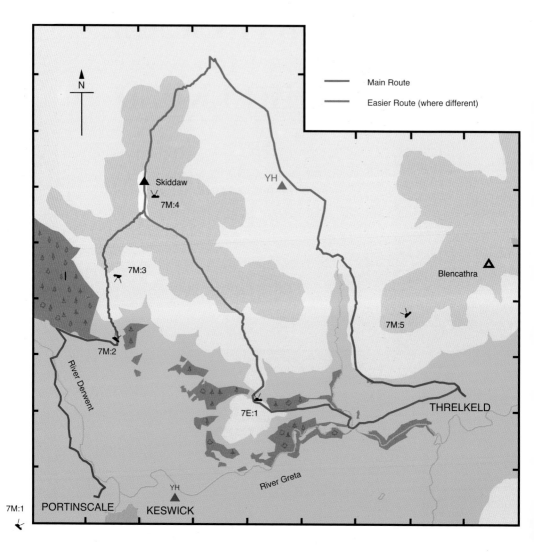

Main Route

Easier Route (where different)

N

Skiddaw
7M:4

YH

Blencathra

7M:3

7M:5

7M:2

River Derwent

7E:1

THRELKELD

River Greta

YH

7M:1
PORTINSCALE
KESWICK

1 km

TIME ALLOWANCE
Main Route: 7½ hours
Easier Route: 7 hours

STARTING LOCATION

Portinscale village, just off the A66(T)/B5289 roads, 2 km (1¼ miles) w of Keswick.
OLM 4/MR 252236.
Virtually no public parking; ask at local hotel (evening meal intention should suffice!)
Start walk on road signed to Derwent Hill and footpath to Keswick.

OVERVIEW/INTEREST

Again a walk of contrasting terrain.
Starts with flat pastureland between Derwent Water and Bassenthwaite Lake.
Route then follows steep slopes of Carl Side to reach the barren Skiddaw summit area.
The trek down is through fells of Skiddaw Forest and includes a stop at the re-opened YH at Skiddaw House.
Stunning views include those of Derwent Water, Longside Edge and Ullock Pike.

FOOTPATHS

Most are good and route finding presents few challenges.
Also wet and boggy areas are virtually non-existent.
Across some of the lower ground the route is somewhat indistinct in places and patience needs to be exercised here to locate the right way.
The steep paths leading to the summit area of Skiddaw are eroded, and in snow/icy conditions the loose slates here can become dangerously slippery.

Statistics	Main route		Easier route	
	Km	**Miles**	**Km**	**Miles**
Distance walked	20.8	13.0	18.2	11.3
	M	**Feet**	**M**	**Feet**
Height climbed	1020	3350	960	3150
Principal Peaks	**M**	**Feet**	**M**	**Feet**
Carl Side	746	2448	746	2448
Skiddaw	931	3053	931	3053

Stage 7 Portinscale to Threlkeld

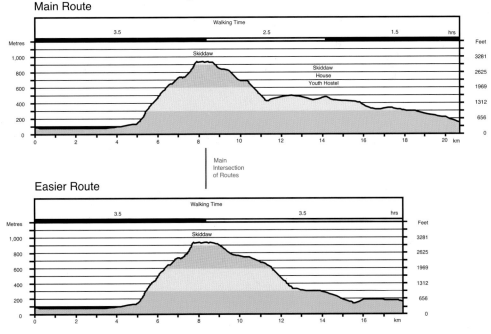

MAIN ROUTE   *(Allow 7½ hours)*

The way to Skiddaw   *(Allow 3½ hours)*

Walk down the road signed to Derwent Hill and footpath to Keswick, passing the village store on your L. On reaching the River Derwent turn L, before the imposing bridge, along the footpath to How Farm and Braithwaite Moss. For some distance this path hugs the w bank of the river and it will take you across the B5289 and A66 (T) roads before leading you round a disused railway line. Near How Farm continue a short distance further along the river bank before using the detour to the N, round the farm buildings.

Still walking N, follow the route of the Allerdale Ramble along the path signed to 'Dancing Gate'. This path runs parallel to the course of the river before converging on it once again. You cross the water here, at High Stock Bridge, about 1½ km (1 mile) (N) of How Farm. Then walk up to the A591 road and turn L along it. After a short distance take the next minor road off on the R, heading marginally uphill towards Millbeck. About 1 km (⅔ mile) further on at Millbeck turn up the gravel track on your L, signed to Skiddaw. Almost immediately select the footpath on your L, again signed to Skiddaw.

7M:1 The silted-up lowlands between Derwent Water and Bassenthwaite Lake overlooked by mighty Skiddaw

7M:2 The gateway to Carl Side at Millbeck

The path rises steeply to give access to the open fells, and in clear weather there are revealing views from here of the challenging upper slopes of Skiddaw and Little Man, far above. Follow the broad grassy path and within 100 paces veer L up the steeper fellside, following a path leading N. After using a P-stile to get across a wire fence, the path becomes stony as views of the Helvellyn Range, Derwent Water and the Central Fells beyond come into sight to your rear. The severe slope leads remorselessly upwards to a brief respite at the craggy outcrop of White Stones. In late August a rich, purple, profusion of heathers smother the otherwise inhospitable slopes hereabouts.

From these rocks a stony, clearly defined, diagonal path leads less steeply upwards, NNE, to even more barren slopes above. The wide, flat summit area of Carl Side is next attained, on which a matching flat cairn is positioned. The dramatic features of Ullock Pike are visible from here to the NW. Beyond the shallow hause below to your R (NE) that accommodates tiny Carlside Tarn, there is a choice of two routes up the final, steep, slopes of Skiddaw. Both of these can become treacherous in severe winter conditions due to the loose slates underfoot, and ascents in snow and ice call for extreme caution. The more distinct route is on the L, eventually veering NNE on a straightforward diagonal. The other is somewhat indistinct to start with, across rough ground ENE, before a narrow but clear

7M:3 The compelling southwards vista from White Stones on Carl Side

7M:4 Approaching the extensive summit area on Skiddaw

route becomes established. This then climbs to the summit ridge in a series of more interesting zigzags. When the weather is clear the views back over Ullock Pike and Longside Edge, now below, are stupendous.

Both paths emerge on the broad summit ridge of Skiddaw near stone shelters. Veer L along this ridge to attain the summit, a short distance further up. The vast summit area of this massive mountain supports several small shelters with a concentration at the top of a summit cairn, a large shelter, a trigonometric point and a commemoration configuration. Weather permitting, the all round panorama from the summit area is superb and in addition to the mountains already recorded, there are excellent views of your continuation route across the high uplands of Skiddaw Forest. In very clear weather the Isle of Man to the wsw and the Solway Firth NNW are also visible.

The way to Skiddaw House Youth Hostel
(Allow 2½ hours)

Start the descent from Skiddaw by walking N past the final shelter situated a short distance below the summit. The ground then falls steeply as your well-established path threads a way through loose slates, before veering to the R (NE). A short

distance further on you will locate a wire fence to your R. This will become a faithful guiding line that will mark your descent across Bakestall and down Birkett Edge to connect you with The Cumbria Way walking route at MR 273313. Always keep to the L of this fence and follow its subtle changes of direction.

This long descent is generally between NE and ENE, in parts down steep, grassy slopes. These are interspersed with more interesting areas of slates and less severe gradients. Towards the end of the descent the fence gives way to a stone wall which leads to The Cumbria Way track. Turn R along this broad track and follow it across the intervening vast rolling fellsides to the sanctuary of the re-opened Youth Hostel at Skiddaw House. This shelter is located some 2½ km (1½ miles) to the SE, from where you first reached The Cumbria Way. Skiddaw House is set in a remote and barren landscape, but its starkness is relieved by an attractive grouping of protective larches.

The way to Threlkeld   *(Allow 1½ hours)*

Continue SE from the Youth Hostel, disengaging yourself from its immediate surrounds by walking through the remains of a dilapidated iron gate and lower down through a gap in a stone wall, situated slightly to your R. After this the path becomes re-established as it bends to the L and leads you down to a bridge across Salehow Beck. The path continues SE to deposit you at the head of Glenderaterra Beck. Further down this feature develops into a narrow steep-sided, V-shaped valley.

Continue to follow the obvious way down the emerging valley as the path veers to the R and southwards. Then further down at a division in the path select the way to your L along the path that turns sharply to the L and which descends towards the valley floor, winding eastwards. The beck is crossed, after which a pleasant, elevated, wide track leads you first S, and then SE round the slope of the fellside to the car parking facilities situated above Blencathra Centre. Walk through the car park and then along the quiet lane that leads down to Threlkeld situated less than 2 km (1¼) miles to the E.

EXTENSIONS FOR STRONG WALKERS
One almost irresistible temptation for strong walkers with a good head for heights is from the top of Skiddaw to traverse E across the high fells of Skiddaw Forest to reach the summit of

7M:5 Skiddaw and Little Man bedecked in winter white, observed from the slopes of Blencathra

Blencathra. Unfortunately such an adventurous route crosses both areas of special scientific interest where access is restricted and also private land across which there are no public rights of way. Therefore, no attempt should be made to reach Blencathra direct from the summit of Skiddaw. Strong walkers who want to do something more are advised to visit Longside Edge and Ullock Pike as part of their ascent of Skiddaw.

EASIER ROUTE   *(Allow 7 hours)*

The way to Skiddaw   *(Allow 3½ hours)*

Use the directions provided in the main route to reach the summit of Skiddaw.

7E:1 Amongst the gentle, rounded foothills of Skiddaw

The way to Threlkeld   *(Allow 3½ hours)*

Start your descent from Skiddaw by using the broad, well-established path leading s and then SE. Continue down this obvious way, to descend round the E flank of Little Man and across the wide spur of Jenkin Hill. From here the well-trodden and eroded route down, steepens appreciably as it veers to the R and follows the course of Whit Beck on your L. The way continues to be straightforward down to the small car park located below at MR 281254. An impressive monumental cross is passed in this descent, in memory of shepherds who bred prize Herdwick sheep and the inscription is particularly poignant. This will remain a secret for you to read yourself.

Now select the path that leads L from the bottom SE end of the car park and follow it to the SE as it curves round the rolling fellside towards a conifer forest. The forest area is skirted to your L. Cross a stile, after which the path swings to the L in the direction of Blencathra. Pass through an iron gate and continue down the ridge to the junction of lanes and tracks at MR 296251. A P-stile provides entry to a lane that you turn L along and then veer R downhill, passing the residence of 'Brundholme'. The way drops to the River Greta and then back up again in a broad loop, and Glenderaterra Beck is crossed at the tip of this. At the top of this next rise you reach the impressive array of buildings located at Wescoe.

Next connect with the footpath to Threlkeld by passing through a K-gate on your L, beyond the buildings. A pleasant walk across undulating meadows now leads you into Threlkeld via Ings, but not before you have negotiated, in quick succession, a wooden gate, two stepped wall stiles, an L-stile, a gate, a further stepped wall stile (be careful to follow the direction of a stone wall to your L here), yet another stepped wall stile, and finally three K-gates at iron and wooden gateways. An attractive block of renovated cottages is passed and beyond these turn R down the lane to reach the village centre.

FURTHER CURTAILMENT

From Millbeck on the outwards route (MR 256262), it is possible to avoid all serious climbing by using the quiet back roads through Applethwaite to reach the car park to the E and then to connect up there with the previously described easier route.

Stage 8
THRELKELD
to
GLENRIDDING

Photograph: Red Tarn and Striding
Edge – Helvellyn

STAGE 8 THRELKELD TO GLENRIDDING

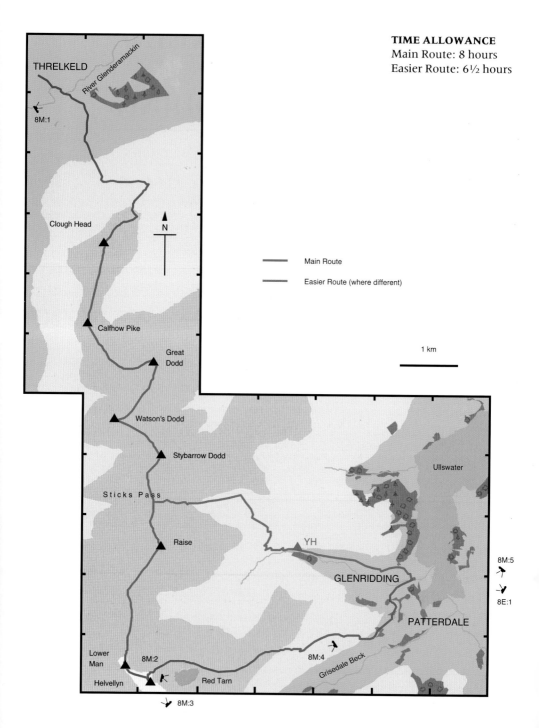

TIME ALLOWANCE
Main Route: 8 hours
Easier Route: 6½ hours

THRELKELD

River Glenderamackin

8M:1

Clough Head

N

Main Route

Easier Route (where different)

1 km

Calfhow Pike

Great
Dodd

Watson's Dodd

Stybarrow Dodd

Sticks Pass

Ullswater

Raise

YH

8M:5

GLENRIDDING

8E:1

PATTERDALE

Lower
Man   8M:2

Helvellyn   Red Tarn   8M:4   Grisedale Beck

8M:3

STARTING LOCATION
Threlkeld village, just off the A66 (T) road, 6 km (3¾ miles) E of Keswick.
OLM 5/MR 321254.
Car park NW of village – holds up to 15 cars.
Start walk on cart track beside St Mary's Church.

OVERVIEW/INTEREST
Starts with flat land through which the river Glenderamackin meanders.
Route then takes in a selection of peaks along the highest and longest N to S groups of mountains in the Lake District.
Peaks covered on the main route are Clough Head, Great Dodd, Watsons's Dodd, Stybarrow Dodd, Raise, Lower Man and Helvellyn.
The trek down to Glenridding is by way of the rocky ridge of Swirral Edge and the N-flanking spur of Grisedale.
Breathtaking views from Helvellyn S towards Striding Edge.
Tiny Lanty's Tarn passed at end of walk.

FOOTPATHS
Care is needed in deciphering the correct route on the initial section to Clough Head: footpaths here are either not clear and/or the ground is severely waterlogged.
There are good, obvious paths from Clough Head, and the scramble down Swirral Edge should pose few problems providing care is exercised on the sound rock.
The final traverse above Grisedale is clear and well drained.

Statistics	Main route		Easier route	
	Km	**Miles**	**Km**	**Miles**
Distance walked	20.6	12.8	16.7	10.4
	M	**Feet**	**M**	**Feet**
Height climbed	1280	4200	900	2950
Principal Peaks	**M**	**Feet**	**M**	**Feet**
Clough Head	726	2381	726	2381
Great Dodd	857	2807	857	2807
Stybarrow Dodd	843	2770	843	2770
Raise	883	2889	—	—
Lower Man	925	3033	—	—
Helvellyn	950	3118	—	—

Stage 8 Threlkeld to Glenridding

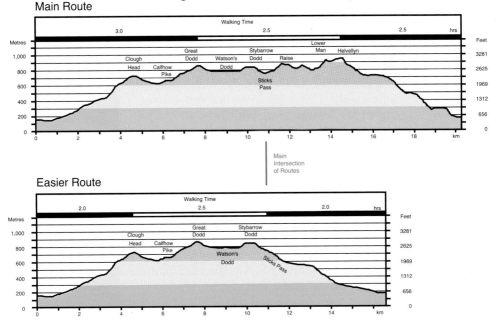

MAIN ROUTE   *(Allow 8 hours)*

The way to Great Dodd   *(Allow 3 hours)*

The cart-track beside St Mary's Church will lead you out of the village and down towards the A66 (T) road. This is achieved by using the P-stile situated a short distance down the track to gain access to a field, and then crossing the field on a diagonal to your L. Cross the busy road with care and continue along the footpath on the opposite side heading towards the outline of the Dodds, far above. Climb the P-stile to your L and walk alongside the River Glenderamackin, with this on your R. Cross a culvert to your R over the wooden footbridge and then the main river by means of the more substantial bridge. Walk along the rising, surfaced lane, go over the disused railway track and head towards the dwelling of 'Newsham'.

Just before reaching 'Newsham' pass through the gate on your R. A short distance on abandon the gravel track, as this disappears further up the fellside into an unpleasant morass, and strike off on a diagonal across open ground heading towards the apex of a copse of trees higher up to your R. Your direction of travel should be ssw. This course will bring you to a wire fence above and beyond the trees. Veer to the L beside this and use this to guide you up through rough, waterlogged ground to the good, gravel track above at a gate. This crosses your direction of approach at right-angles. Turn L here and walk E along the broad track snaking uphill round Hausewell Brow. By now, in favourable weather, you will have clear, unimpeded views of the massive shapes of Skiddaw and Blencathra across the wide intervening valley to the NW.

Be careful now to gain access to the steeply rising fellside on your R at the second P-stile. This is positioned about 1 km (⅔ mile) along the gravel track from your point of entry. A stiff climb sw up the steep fellside now follows. Walk towards the brow of the sweeping, grassy fellside heading towards the R (w) of the outcrop of rocks named White Pike. The slope progressively steepens and towards the top of the ridge veer to your L, towards and through s, making a final diagonal approach to reach the crag of White Pike that avoids the steepest, roughest ground on your L. White Pike is positioned at MR 339229 and a cairn marks the spot.

From here head wsw up to Clough Head, situated at the top of the next grassy slope. In misty weather be vigilant here as there is a dangerous edge on your R above Red Screes. Should you reach this, veer to the L (ssw) along it and this will lead you up

to the vicinity of Clough Head, now to your L. At Clough Head you will find a trigonometric point and a small shelter. Also, in all but the most atrocious weather conditions, your navigational problems should now ease as there are distinct paths from here that lead all the way across the Dodds to the far-off summit of Helvellyn. In fact, route-finding now literally becomes a bit of a 'doddle'!

Start the next part of the walk by heading SW along the path that descends across the rounded grassy fellside, develops into a cart-track, and eventually rises to the jumble of rocks that form Calfhow Pike. From this craggy summit head SSE, still climbing up the rounded fellsides along the convenient cart-track. Keep to the L of some nasty peat hags, before your way curves progressively to the L, climbing steadily, to attain the final broad, sparsely grassed, higher slopes of Great Dodd. These are scaled on a ENE heading.

8M:1 A distant view of the Dodds far beyond Causey Pike

The way to Helvellyn   *(Allow 2½ hours)*

At the summit of Great Dodd make a 90 degrees turn to your R before descending SE for a short distance to reach a circular, stone shelter just below the top. At this shelter trim your direction of travel to SSW, and walk along the gently sloping, grassy track that veers first SW and finally towards W to Watson's Dodd. (There is a direct main path S that by-passes this flattish summit area, to the L.)

From Watson's Dodd turn through 45 degrees and walk back to the main path now heading SE. This obvious path then climbs towards Stybarrow Dodd. Again the main route S avoids the interesting summit area, but a short climb up the grassy fellside on your L will bring you to the summit shelter. Descend to the S to rejoin the main path. This then drops to the apex of Sticks Pass at MR 343182, after negotiating some waterlogged ground.

Beyond the pass the terrain rises again up the craggy slopes of Raise as your route continues southwards. The path threads a way through the craggy outcrops of exposed, pitted rock in a series of zigzags, ever upwards, to reach the equally rocky summit area of Raise. These serrated and irregular outlines provide good frames for photographing the distant fells, and are in stark contrast to the rounded, grassy domes of the Dodds previously encountered.

8M:2 Red Tarn and Striding Edge as seen from the summit of Helvellyn

8M:3 Helvellyn and Striding Edge observed from a snow-capped Fairfield

The way continues ssw, descending marginally, and in good weather views of Helvellyn and its famous arêtes of Swirral Edge and Striding Edge appear ahead. Thirlmere lies below in the great fault-line to the w. Whiteside Bank is next left behind as the stony path first drops down before climbing ssw to the summit of Lower Man. After this the path obligingly sweeps round up a broad L hand curve to the SE to gain the vast area of level ground on the summit of Helvellyn. The several features of this massive mountain top are worth your passing inspection, and from this high level viewing platform the following major fells beyond the Helvellyn range itself are revealed, weather conditions permitting: the Coniston Fells, Crinkle Crags, Bow Fell and the Scafells, Great Gable and Pillar group, High Stile group, the NW fells including Grasmoor and Grisedale Pike, Skiddaw, Blencathra, the easterly fells including the High Street configuration, and the Fairfield Horseshoe.

The way to Glenridding   *(Allow 2½ hours)*

When you are ready to descend along Swirral Edge, head N from the trigonometric point for about 150 paces to locate the small cairn marking the top of this arête along the eroded, easterly face of Helvellyn. During the scramble down keep to the crest of the ridge descending over firm rock, where there are conveniently positioned, secure hand and foot holds. There are several ways down discrete sections of the arête so choose the one that suits your capabilities and appetite for exposure best. Do not, however, be tempted to drop to the looser steep, scree slope to your R as this can be treacherous.

At the end of the jumbled rocky sections a clearly defined stony path steers a way down to the R to reach lower, more sheltered ground. When the path divides, choose the lower, R-hand branch and follow this down to skirt Red Tarn below. Cross Red Tarn Beck and traverse across the peaty grasslands to gain the ridge ahead at the location of Hole-in-the-Wall, MR 359155. Cross the stone wall by the L-stile and follow the eroded path diagonally down to the E towards Grisedale. Continue to descend, ignoring a path off to the L just prior to passing through a gateway.

After negotiating a K-gate, about 100 metres above the valley floor, select the path on your L that skirts the conifer trees and climbs up the bracken-laden fellside. This way will soon lead you through a K-gate, upwards to the secluded waters of tiny Lanty's Tarn, an oasis of tranquillity and beauty nestling beneath its protective canopy of enclosing conifers. At the far end of the tarn another K-gate is encountered, and beyond this, a zigzag path to the L leads through more gates, across a bridge over the brow of the fell and then steeply down to the lane below. This new descent route from the tarn is marked by yellow arrowheads. Turn R along the lane and this will lead you by the side of Glenridding Beck down into the centre of the village.

EXTENSIONS FOR STRONG WALKERS

The obvious extension for walkers with a head for heights is from the Hole-in-the-Wall location to climb back to the top of Helvellyn along Striding Edge. The only slight problem then is that you will have to use either this arête or come down Swirral Edge for a second time to arrive back at Hole-in-the-Wall again in order to continue along the main route.

Another extension is from the end of Swirral Edge to climb Catstye Cam. You can then manoeuvre back down round Red Tarn to rejoin the main route, or descend down the steep, more demanding, N slopes of Catstye Cam to the remote and wild cove at its base. Afterwards you use the track descending to the NE to connect with the easier route continuing down Glenridding at MR 363174.

One other possibility is from the summit of Helvellyn to continue along the ridge S over Nethermost Pike and Dollywaggon Pike down to Grisedale Tarn. At the tarn turn NE and use the popular route down Grisedale to link up with the main route S of Lanty's Tarn at MR 380159.

8M:4 Descending from the rigours of Striding Edge into tranquil Grisedale

EASIER ROUTE   *(Allow 6½ hours)*

The way to Clough Head   *(Allow 2 hours)*

Use the directions given for the main route to reach Clough Head.

The way to Sticks Pass   *(Allow 2½ hours)*

Continue to follow the directions provided in the main route to arrive at the top of Sticks Pass, MR 343182.

8M:5 A view from Place Fell of Patterdale and Grisedale with their encircling high mountainous landscape

The way to Glenridding *(Allow 2 hours)*

Turn sharp L at Sticks Pass and descend E along the narrow but well-defined track. This leads for about 1½ km (1 mile), almost due E, gradually descending along the remote valley beside the course of Sticks Gill. The stream is eventually crossed within the confines of some unsightly abandoned quarry spoil workings, before the way turns SE to reach the extensively mined area around Stang End. A surprisingly steep descent now follows, over boulders, stones and debris from disused workings and you are rightly warned to keep to the designated route through this terrain, to avoid further disturbing the unstable slopes in this area.

Safely at the bottom, the route continues ESE along a broad track that is upgraded to Greenside Road as it continues down the N flank of Glenridding past the YH and above the beck. This leads into the village some 2½ km (1½ miles) further on.

FURTHER CURTAILMENT
The climb onto the Dodds is both strenuous and not straightforward. This relatively difficult section can be avoided by first walking to Threlkeld Bridge (MR 315247), and just SW of there picking up the well-signed and upgraded pathways down the W flank of St John's in the Vale to reach the W end of Sticks Pass at MR 318189. This is a short distance S of the YH. Unfortunately, you will have to walk by the side of either the main A591 and/or B5322 road(s), depending on which particular route you select, for your final approach to the pass. Turn L and head ESE up the pass to connect with the easier route at the top.

8E:1 The long descent into Glenridding from lofty Sticks Pass observed from Place Fell

Stage 9

GLENRIDDING
to
TROUTBECK

Photograph: Looking across Patterdale
towards Helvellyn

STAGE 9 GLENRIDDING TO TROUTBECK

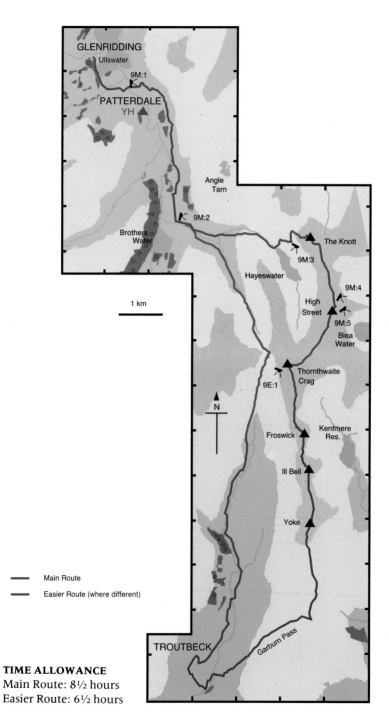

GLENRIDDING
Ullswater
9M:1
PATTERDALE
YH

Angle
Tarn
9M:2
Brothers
Water

Hayeswater

The Knott
9M:3

9M:4
High
Street
9M:5
Blea
Water

1 km

Thornthwaite
Crag
9E:1

N

Froswick
Kentmere
Res.

Ill Bell

Yoke

Main Route
Easier Route (where different)

TROUTBECK
Garburn Pass

TIME ALLOWANCE
Main Route: 8½ hours
Easier Route: 6½ hours

STARTING LOCATION

Glenridding village, on w shore of Ullswater, on A592 road.

OLM 5/MR 386169.

Extensive car parking facilities in village.

Start walk on A592 road, heading s towards Patterdale.

OVERVIEW/INTEREST

A walk dominated by the rounded peaks of the remote easterly fells.

Peaks covered on route: The Knott, High Street, Thornthwaite Crag, Froswick, Ill Bell and Yoke.

Lower land at beginning and end embraces attractive blend of villages, farms and woodlands.

Possible wildlife sightings: wild ponies and eagles.

FOOTPATHS

In the main very good, apart from the long descent on the easier route.

This descent, in places, is both waterlogged and not all that easy to follow. There are a few other significant waterlogged areas to cross and the occasional spot where care has to be exercised to keep along the correct route.

No serious erosion on any of the paths used.

Statistics	Main route		Easier route	
	Km	**Miles**	**Km**	**Miles**
Distance walked	23.1	14.3	17.4	10.8
	M	**Feet**	**M**	**Feet**
Height climbed	1140	3740	620	2030
Principal Peaks	**M**	**Feet**	**M**	**Feet**
The Knott	739	2423	—	—
High Street	828	2718	—	—
Thornthwaite Crag	784	2569	—	—
Ill Bell	757	2476	—	—
Threshthwaite Mouth	—	—	600	1970

Stage 9 Glenridding to Troutbeck

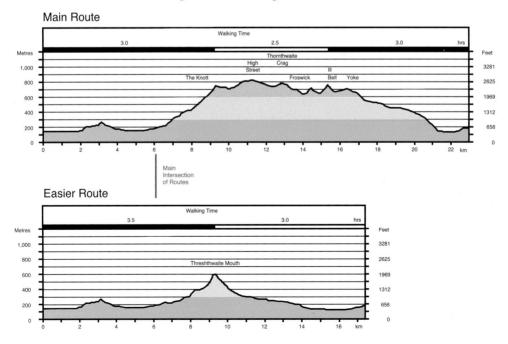

117

MAIN ROUTE   *(Allow 8½ hours)*

The way to The Knott   *(Allow 3 hours)*

Walk s on the A592 towards Patterdale, using the permitted paths beside this busy road wherever possible. At the school in Patterdale turn L down the track to Side Farm, possibly to be greeted by inquisitive ponies asking with their eyes 'Have you come for a ride?'. Pass between the farm buildings and turn R down the footpath to Hartsop. Less than ½ km (⅓ mile) further on you will come to a small cluster of dwellings at MR 401162. Pass through the gateway on your L here and walk up the open fell to reach the main path a short distance above, that circles the western, lower slopes of Place Fell. Veer to the R along this.

The path traverses up the fell along a comfortable gradient but no sooner do unrestricted, interesting views begin to appear on your R than you have to select the branch in the path to the R that leads you above Crookabeck farm and then back down the fellside to rejoin the main path s along the valley at MR 405146. From here follow the obvious, well-signed, lower path to Hartsop. It is not long before the path brings you to the village at Langton Adventure Centre, where you turn L. Hartsop is a really delightful village of attractive, irregularly positioned houses and the justifiable reason for guiding you along the lower valley path is to give you the opportunity to walk right through this charming hamlet.

9M:1 Imminent confrontation at Side Farm, Patterdale

9M:2 Approaching the delightful village of Hartsop

At the far end of the village you will come to a sizeable car park and at the far end of this a K-gate provides entry to the bridleway to Hayeswater. Initially keep to the surfaced track, ignoring a grassy way down on your R. After passing through a gateway take the broad gravel path on your R that descends to cross Hayeswater Gill. The path then rises and avoids private land ahead by turning sharp L. The way then climbs eastwards in the lee of the lower slopes of Gray Crag to reach the remote and well-concealed tarn of Hayeswater.

Cross the exit stream of Hayeswater Gill immediately below the retaining dam, pass through the gap in the stone wall and climb up the steep slope, first to the NE but then veering to the ESE. The official path is then along two long traverses, the first to your R and then a back-track to the L. These continue to gain height at a more comfortable rate and they will bring you to the main ridge. Turn R and continue to climb. A short distance further on, your way intersects with a better established route coming up from Angle Tarn.

The main path leads round, and below, The Knott and therefore just beyond a dilapidated stone wall turn R and use the line of this wall to guide you SSE up the grassy fell along an intermittent path. The summit is soon reached and the flattish, grassy top is a little disappointing, being featureless save for a large pyramid-shaped cairn. However, weather permitting, the views more than compensate for this. On a clear day Martindale and Boredale are visible to the N, Rampsgill Head and Kidsty Pike to the E, the High Street configuration with the pronounced beacon of Thornthwaite Crag in view to the S, Stony Cove Pike and Red Screes to the SW, the Fairfield and Helvellyn groups with the highest peaks of the Central Fells popping up beyond them to the W and the faint outlines of Skiddaw and Blencathra far away to the NW. Most of this superb mountain panorama will be in view for the rest of the day.

The way to Ill Bell   *(Allow 2½ hours)*

Leave The Knott to the ESE to regain the main path a short distance below. Turn R along this, heading S towards High Street. Continue along the ridge and when the path divides keep to the L-hand one, nearest to the edge of the high ground as this provides the better unrestricted views to the E: these are of the long rocky spur of Riggindale Crag, Harter Fell and Haweswater

9M:3 Looking down on Hayeswater

9M:4 Riggindale spur leading the eyes down to Haweswater Reservoir

Reservoir. Further up locate the cairn marking the top of Riggindale Crag and in clear weather descend a short way down the slope to your L to observe the quite spectacular view down over the high level combe that traps Blea Water. Ill Bell and Yoke are also visible, as is the coastline on very clear days.

Retrace your final steps, traverse to the L and walk uphill to rejoin the path. Follow this beside the stone wall to the summit of High Street. Sometimes along here you will disturb a group of shaggy, wild ponies and their inquisitive but ungainly appearance is somewhat out of character with the name of the ground they are contentedly grazing on, for these final approach slopes of High Street are designated 'Racecourse Hill'! The surface of the flat summit is only broken by man-made features and the protruding shoulders of the mountain block most of the long-distance views.

Continue ssw from High Street, descending gradually beside the crumbling stone wall, to the shallow hause ahead. Avoid all forks leading off to the L. Instead veer round to the R at the hause and head sw to converge with the main, quite badly eroded, wide path connecting the High Street ridge with

Thornthwaite Crag. Veer L down this and then follow its graceful R-hand curve upwards to the summit of Thornthwaite Crag and the large beacon situated there. Additional sightings from here could include Nan Bield Pass, Kentmere Pike, a more revealing view of your continuation route over Froswick, Ill Bell and Yoke, as well as Windermere, Wansfell Pike, the Coniston Fells, and more certain identification of the Langdale Pikes, Crinkle Crags and the Scafells.

Leave Thornthwaite Crag down the path to the SSE, and keep to the edge of the ridge on your L as a preliminary to crossing the shallow hause linking Thornthwaite Crag and Froswick. Climb the zigzag path to your L to reach the summit of Froswick. Continue to walk southwards and a further quick down and up will bring you to the top of the higher peak of Ill Bell (not to be confused with Mardale Ill Bell!). After climbing through the morass of jumbled rocks that form the higher slopes of Ill Bell there are three summit cairns inviting your inspection at the top.

The way to Troutbeck   *(Allow 3 hours)*

Another descent, still to the S, follows but then veer SSE to cross the broad expanse of Yoke, ignoring a branch path to your R that leads more directly towards Windermere. Further down, head for the craggy outcrop on which a cairn is positioned, and as the way down steepens cross a wall by a L-stile. Use the continuation of this wall as a guide, keeping it in sight to your L during the rest of your descent to the Garburn Pass Bridleway. The final section before connecting with the well-used bridleway is a bit trying, for the terrain here is waterlogged and there are several, indeterminate, intermittent paths here. However, keep descending to the S, and in your final approach walk down one of several paths that veers away from the wall to the R to reach Garburn Pass between MR 434044 and MR 437044.

9M:5 Sun-rays dancing on the surface of Blea Water with Harter Fell looking on approvingly

Turn R along the broad, stony and in this vicinity, quite bumpy pass. The route than veers to the L round Moor Head as you continue to surrender height. Keep to the Garburn track for about 1½ km (1 mile) and then locate and follow a steep, grassy traverse to your R. At the bottom of this diagonal, select the lower path, ahead on the L and negotiate a gateway. Pass above the Haybarn Inn and take the road on your R leading through Limefitt Caravan Park.

At the far end of the caravan site, the camp road leads over the river (Trout Beck) to the main A592 road. Turn L along this road and walk down the short distance to Jesus Church, Troutbeck. Inside, the church is delightfully simple, apart from the exquisite

stained glass windows. After looking around the church, turn down the bridleway on the N side of the church yard, keep to the L at two junctions of paths ahead, and after passing through a gateway, a narrow path will lead you to the sprawling hamlet of Troutbeck.

EXTENSIONS FOR STRONG WALKERS
From Thornthwaite Crag it is feasible to use the longer, more demanding eastern flank of The Kentmere Horseshoe for the descent route. This is achieved by first circling eastwards above Bleathwaite Crag to the summit of Mardale Ill Bell. Then using the craggy Nan Bield Pass to the SE to reach Harter Fell. From here the descent is southwards over Kentmere Pike to Kentmere. (Be careful in your final approach to the village to leave the main ridge to the NE of Kentmere at MR 472067 and to descend along the less-used diagonal path that leads down to Hallow Bank.) At Kentmere make for the church and after walking up the lane from this to the NW, the Garburn Pass rising to the W will connect you back onto the main route which was previously described.

EASIER ROUTE   *(Allow 6½ hours)*

The way to Threshthwaite Mouth   *(Allow 3½ hours)*

[This particular variant is considered to be easier than the suggested main route only in terms of height climbed and consequentially in reduced exposure! In clear weather conditions the main route is considered to be vastly more enjoyable than this alternative route.]

Use the directions provided for the main route to reach the car park at the far end of Hartsop Village at MR 410131. After passing through the ᴋ-gate turn sharp ʀ through the immediate gateway and walk along the footpath signed to Pasture Beck. Cross the stream and follow the path round the lower slopes of the steep Hartsop Dodd spur, walking sᴇ, to arrive at the entrance to the valley of Pasture Bottom. From here, to subvert rugby parlance, it is one long 'up and over'. The path first rises gradually but steadily to the w of Pasture Beck, before steeper gradients are encountered at Threshthwaite Cove. The final climb up the steep, rocky fellside to reach the hause of Threshthwaite Mouth is quite demanding. This high point of the easier route is a convenient spot to stop for refreshments.

The way to Troutbeck   *(Allow 3 hours)*

The descent has similar characteristics to the way up, but this time the hard work is dealt with first in climbing down the steep and craggy upper slopes along Park Fell Head. At Threshthwaite Mouth hause keep to the ʀ near to the craggy, shattered, boulder strewn slopes of Threshthwaite Crag. From here a faint grassy track leads down ssᴇ, more or less in-line with the distant summits of Froswick and Ill Bell. Beware of holes in this path!

Lower down, the gradient decreases as the route continues along the track beside Trout Beck through erratic boulders and across boggy areas. There are intermittent cairns to guide walkers along a path that is obviously not well used. The way then leads down a grassy spur and a stream is crossed by turning ʀ at the head of a shallow ravine and above a miniature waterfall (at MR 424093). After passing through a gate breaching a stone wall, be careful to keep to the ʀ flank of the valley, thus avoiding marshy ground and crossing the beck again until much lower down. Eventually, a wooden stile provides the only crossing of a stone wall lying at right angles to your direction of approach, and this important feature gives access to more enclosed and sheltered landscape.

9E:1 The long trek southwards from Threshthwaite Mouth to Troutbeck revealed from the commanding heights of Thornthwaite Crag

The way then leads over quite unpleasant, waterlogged ground, down to a re-crossing of Trout Beck, this time by means of a substantial stone footbridge situated at MR 418067. Further progress southwards is along a broad loop to the L to pass Hird Wood, before the path descends to the farmstead and dwellings of Troutbeck Park. Keep to the R of the farm buildings in your initial approach and then turn sharp L to pass in front of the white cottages. Watch out for a not too friendly welcome from dogs here! A surfaced lane leads further down the valley and Hag Gill is crossed before re-crossing Trout Beck once again, on this occasion at Ing Bridge. Continue s along Ing Lane towards Town Head. Take a L turning up a bridleway that leads to the main A592 road, cross this road and the lane opposite will lead you into the straggling village of Troutbeck.

FURTHER CURTAILMENT
No further curtailments are obvious.

Stage 10
TROUTBECK
to
GRASMERE

Photograph: Looking down from the
slopes of Wansfell Pike towards
Ambleside, with Bow Fell and the
Langdale Pikes in the distance

STAGE 10 TROUTBECK TO GRASMERE

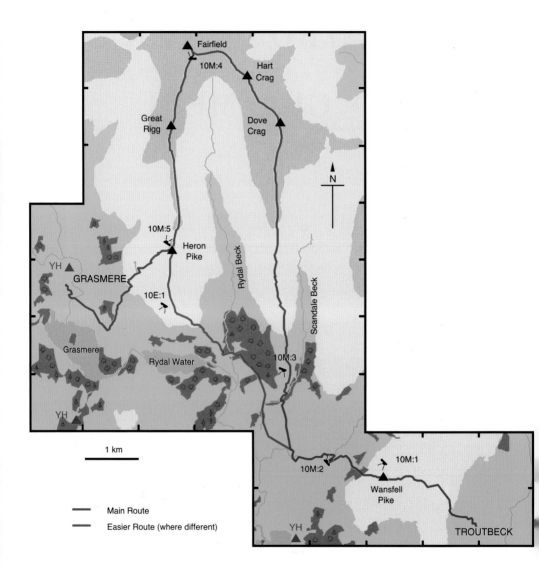

TIME ALLOWANCE
Main Route: 8 hours
Easier Route: 6 hours

STARTING LOCATION

Troutbeck village, lies just off the A592, 4 km (2½ miles) E of Ambleside.
OLM 7/MR 411035.
No public car park in village; ask at local hotel. Start walk on Nanny Lane at side of Lanefoot Farm, MR 410034.

OVERVIEW/INTEREST

The walk is divided into two parts.
First, the climb to Wansfell Pike followed by descent into Ambleside via the spectacular falls of Stock Ghyll.
Second, the climb, from Ambleside, on to the famous Fairfield Horseshoe, achieving the peaks of Dove Crag, Hart Crag, Fairfield, Great Rigg and Heron Pike.
Panoramic vistas of distant mountain groupings.
The delightful Alcock Tarn is visited and walk finishes near Wordsworth's Dove Cottage.

FOOTPATHS

Save for some waterlogged stretches on the long spur up to Dove Crag, footpaths are on the whole very good.
Patches of erosion, particularly on the top part of the descent from Wansfell Pike.
Route finding is straightforward and established paths are nearly always obvious.
The start of the descent from Heron Pike is down open fellsides with no continuous distinct route, but this stretch is soon covered.

Statistics	Main route		Easier route	
	Km	**Miles**	**Km**	**Miles**
Distance walked	20.9	13.0	13.5	8.4
	M	**Feet**	**M**	**Feet**
Height climbed	1250	4100	870	2860
Principal Peaks	**M**	**Feet**	**M**	**Feet**
Wansfell Pike	484	1581	484	1581
Dove Crag	792	2603	—	—
Hart Crag	822	2698	—	—
Fairfield	873	2863	—	—
Great Rigg	766	2513	—	—
Heron Pike	612	2003	612	2003

Stage 10 Troutbeck to Grasmere

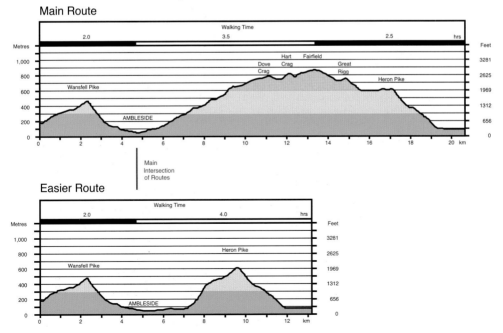

MAIN ROUTE   *(Allow 8 hours)*

The way to Ambleside   *(Allow 2 hours)*

Nanny Lane is a stony track leading steeply up the fellside, and starting with several right-angled turns. The worst is soon over as the gradient declines and the lane becomes established as a pleasant, stone and grassy way between retaining stone walls. After about 1 km (⅔ mile) look out for an iron к-gate and stile on your L, pass through these and follow the footpath signed 'Ambleside via Wansfell'.

A clear, recently renovated path ascends wnw across acid moorland to the summit of Wansfell Pike. There are many revealing views from here including the Coniston Fells, looking up the two Langdale valleys to the Central Fells, and of perhaps more immediate interest the general configuration of the Fairfield Horseshoe is revealed. There are also sightings of the easterly fells including Red Screes, Stony Cove Pike, Thornthwaite Crag, part of the High Street range and the long Ill Bell spur radiating s. Many walkers, including the author, also consider this peak provides one of the finest views down the length of Windermere.

10M:1 Sunset observed from the summit of Wansfell Pike

10M:2 Stockghyll Force

Cross the wire fence at the L-stile, exercising care not to be tripped by the questionable iron bar positioned at the top! Walk to the rocky outcrop ahead. From here descend the clearly defined, quite badly eroded path to the WNW towards Ambleside. Further below, the way bends to the R round a small copse of beech trees. After this the path is down steep grass slopes, and this section terminates at the end of a walled lane, the entrance to which is blocked by a fallen tree that has become a semipermanent feature here.

Climb the L-stile over the opposite wall and continue downhill. Next a P-stile, followed by an iron ladder, gives access to a surfaced lane that you turn L down. A short distance further on, after crossing a cattle grid, turn R along a fenced path near to a sign indicating a public footpath to 'Kirkstone 3½'. Enter the enclosed area of Stock Ghyll at an impressive iron turnstile, and veer R uphill along the internal pathways. Cross the stream at the wooden bridge above the cascading waters and descend on the N bank of the falls. There are some quite superb viewing positions along here, and the majority of these are obvious. Recross the beck further down and turn R, following the path back to the surfaced lane. Turn R and walk down to Ambleside.

The way to Fairfield   *(Allow 3½ hours)*

At Ambleside, on approaching the hustle and bustle below, turn R passing round The Salutation Inn. Escape from the busy main street by turning R again, this time along North Road and recross Stock Ghyll before passing The Unicorn Inn. Veer R for a short distance along the road to Kirkstone, named Smithy Brow at this point, and take the next turning to your L down Sweden Bridge Lane. This leads you, about 1 km (⅔ mile) further on, to Nook End Farm, the gateway to the open fells once again.

Pass through the tidy farmyard, and then keep to the lower path that crosses Low Sweden Bridge. The way then curves upwards to the R and further height is gained as the wide, gravel path passes through conveniently spaced gaps in several stone walls that render the L-stiles there redundant. Eventually a zigzag to the L leads up to the craggy ridge and a choice of good, distinct paths lead either up or round the outcrops of Low and then High Pikes. Your direction of travel is now due N. The route continues to the W of Thack Bottom Edge, and this leads to the more exposed, less steep slopes that rise to the summit of Dove Crag. Some boggy, clinging peat hags have to be crossed up here, and after prolonged rain these will exercise your skills at locating continuously firm stepping positions.

From Dove Crag the direction of the route changes to NW as the going becomes more rocky and the ascent and descent of Hart Crag along the cairned, well-drained, steeper path makes a welcome change from the waterlogged slopes further down. From the summit of Hart Crag a pronounced col has to be crossed, appropriately named Link Hause, to gain the wide, higher band of flattish fellside that then leads w to the summit of Fairfield, now less than 1 km (⅔ mile) away. The many deep chasms together with the bewildering array of craggy outcrops and rocky ridges that line the N rim of Fairfield make compelling viewing.

The huge rounded summit area of Fairfield supports several viewing platforms, some of which you need to descend to in order to observe all that this strategically positioned fell has to reveal. The areas well worth your attention include, the N cairn for views along Cofa Pike and St Sunday Crag, the westerly edge for the revelations of the Central Massif of the Lakeland Fells protruding over the nearer bulk of Seat Sandal, and the cross shelter for the spectacular scenery flanking the remote, glaciated valley of Deepdale with its extensive drumlins.

[AUTHOR'S NOTE: The National Park rangers have pointed out that Fairfield is a very exposed mountain, and in misty conditions walkers can easily become confused when exploring its vast summit area, particularly when they are being buffeted by strong winds! Therefore only linger here in favourable weather, and always take frequent compass bearings in this vicinity to check your exact position and to confirm your next intended direction of travel!]

10M:3 Sharing a view back towards Ambleside and Windermere!

10M:4 A hurried departure from the frozen summit of Fairfield

The way to Grasmere   *(Allow 2½ hours)*

Leave the summit area of Fairfield along the broad spur to the sw, walking down the wide path of the gentle slope. The way veers towards s as Great Rigg is scaled. The direction then passes through s, along the narrowing ridge where some 2 km (1¼ miles) further on down the undulating crest of the massive spur, the craggy summit of Heron Pike is reached. During this section of the walk, in favourable lighting conditions, no less than nine stretches of water are simultaneously visible; see if you can spot and name them all! No prizes for this though.

Leave the main ridge at Heron Pike and drop down the steep slope on your R crossing the rough fellside. Your direction is generally sw, and this should be trimmed towards Alcock Tarn when it becomes visible below over the protruding shoulder of the intervening fellside. Intermittent paths down soon appear and select one that leads directly to the tarn. Alcock Tarn supports abundant plant and animal life, and therefore presents an interesting and sheltered spot to linger at for refreshments.

Walk round the s tip of the tarn and continue down the well-established footpaths leading sw to reach the minor road below at How Top. Veer R down this, and after passing Dove Cottage and rubbing shoulders with the Wordsworth fraternity, cross the main A591 road and use the B5287 loop road to reach the centre of Grasmere.

EXTENSIONS FOR STRONG WALKERS

There is one obvious extension, and this is to complete the full Fairfield Horseshoe route by continuing along the main spur from Heron Pike and using this to descend by way of Lord Crag and Nab Scar into Rydal. From Rydal there are obvious, well-used routes either N of Rydal Water and E of Grasmere Lake, or alternatively S of Rydal Water and W of Grasmere Lake that will take you into Grasmere Village through pleasant, wooded, lowland scenery.

EASIER ROUTE   *(Allow 6 hours)*

The way to Ambleside   *(Allow 2 hours)*

Ambleside is reached by following the directions given for the main route.

The way to Grasmere   *(Allow 4 hours)*

Leave Ambleside by the main A591 road walking NW in the direction of Rydal. Within 1 km (⅔ mile) of the village, at MR 372052, turn R through the impressive wrought iron gates along the footpath signed to Rydal Hall. This leads round attractive parkland containing a large variety of specimen trees including oak, sycamore, larch, ash, beech and chestnut. Bisect the outbuildings of the hall and continue along the main path over level ground, crossing Rydal Beck in the process.

10M:5 Hardy walkers braving the winter hazards of completing the Fairfield Horseshoe

10E:1 The snow-capped Coniston and Central Fells observed beyond Rydal Water and Grasmere Lake

The lane will bring you to a surfaced road that you turn R up to pass Rydal Mount. This is where Wordsworth lived from 1813 to 1850. Continue uphill and pass through a gate-less opening in a stone wall. Next choose the path diagonally ahead to your L that leads more steeply uphill beyond a K-gate. Apart from avoiding a branch path off on the L under an ash tree, the obvious route continues to climb by means of a series of alternating zigzags and traverses. This part of the way is only obstructed by a solitary L-stile. These steep, unremitting slopes are probably the most demanding section of this stage of the route. Fortunately their severe gradient declines as the route bends round in a gentle curve through N and over Lord Crag to the summit of Heron Pike. From here follow the directions provided in the main route to descend via Alcock Tarn to Grasmere Village.

FURTHER CURTAILMENT
From Rydal Hall it is feasible to avoid the steep exhausting climb up Nab Scar by selecting one of several lower routes round the lakes of Rydal Water and Grasmere. There are clearly identified alternatives above either the N or the S shoreline of Rydal Water, and variations are possible along each of these two curtailments. All of these ways are through delightful, lowland, pastoral scenery, and the views across each of the two lakes are enchanting.

ACCOMMODATION

Finding suitable, value-for-money overnight accommodation with minimum effort is a significant factor in the overall enjoyment of The Lakeland Round. For this reason a suitable accommodation register is provided for each of the selected overnight stops along the route.

TABLE 6   **ACCOMMODATION REGISTER**

STAGE: 1
Grasmere to Coniston

Kelvyn & Lesley Higgins
ASH COTTAGE
Red Lion Square
Grasmere
Cumbria LA22 9SP
Tel: (015394) 35224

The Sweeney Family
THE TRAVELLERS REST INN
Grasmere
Cumbria LA22 9RR
Tel: (015394) 35604

Mrs A Dixon
OAK LODGE
Easedale Road
Grasmere
Cumbria LA22 9QS
Tel: (015394) 35527

RYELANDS
Grasmere
Cumbria LA22 9SU
Tel: (015394) 35757

Mr & Mrs P Nelson
UNDERCRAG
Easedale Road
Grasmere
Cumbria
Tel: (015394) 35349

Ken & Olive Smith
SILVER LEA
Easedale Road
Grasmere
Cumbria
Tel: (015394) 35657

STAGES: 1 & 2
Grasmere to Coniston to Elterwater

BLACK BULL INN & HOTEL
Yewdale Road
Coniston
Cumbria LA21 8DU
Tel: (015394) 41335/ 41668

SUN HOTEL & COACHING INN
Coniston
Cumbria LA21 8HQ
Tel: (015394) 41248

THE YEWDALE HOTEL
Yewdale Road
Coniston
Cumbria LA21 8DU
Tel: (015394) 41280

Mr and Mrs G Cross
WATERHEAD COUNTRY GUEST HOUSE
Waterhead
Coniston
Cumbria LA21 8AJ
Tel: (015394) 41442

Mrs Mary M Purdy
OAKLANDS
Yewdale Road
Coniston
Cumbria LA21 8DX
Tel: (015394) 41245

Mrs Lilian Grant
CRUACHAN
Collingwood Close
Coniston
Cumbria LA22 8DZ
Tel: (015394) 41628

Mrs Christine Hartshorn
SHEPHERDS VILLA
Coniston
Cumbria LA21 8EE
Tel: (015394) 41337

STAGES: 2 & 3
Coniston to Elterwater to Wasdale Head

THE BRITANNIA INN
Elterwater
Ambleside
Cumbria LA22 9HP
Tel: (015394) 37210

THE ELTERMERE HOTEL
Elterwater
Ambleside
Cumbria LA22 9HY
Tel: (015394) 37207

Mr & Mrs M Riley
BARNHOWE
Elterwater
Ambleside
Cumbria LA22 9HW
Tel: (015394) 37346

Mrs M E Rice
FELLSIDE
3 & 4 Lane End
Elterwater
Ambleside
Cumbria
Tel: (015394) 37678

Mrs D Brown
LANGSTRATH
Chapel Stile
Ambleside
Cumbria LA22 9JJ
Tel: (015394) 37262

Mr & Mrs A Beavon
SOUTH VIEW
Chapel Stile
Ambleside
Cumbria
Tel: (015394) 37248

STAGES: 3 & 4
Elterwater to
Wasdale Head to
Buttermere

WASDALE HEAD INN
Wasdale Head
Gosforth
Cumbria CA20 1EX
Tel: (019467) 26229

Mrs A Buchannon
BURNTHWAITE FARM
Wasdale Head
Gosforth
Cumbria CA20 1EX
Tel: (019467) 26242

Mrs J Preston
WASDALE HEAD HALL
FARM
Wasdale Head
Gosforth
Cumbria CA20 1EX
Tel: (019467) 26245

Mrs C Naylor
ROW HEAD FARM
Wasdale Head
Gosforth
Cumbria CA20 1EX
Tel: (019467) 26244

Mrs S Naylor
MIDDLE ROW
Wasdale Head
Gosforth
Cumbria CA20 1EX
Tel: (019467) 26306

STAGES: 4 & 5
Wasdale Head to
Buttermere to
Braithwaite

Peter and Janet
McGuire
THE BRIDGE HOTEL
Buttermere
Via Cockermouth
Cumbria CA13 9UZ
Tel: (017687) 70252

Mr and Mrs John
Richardson
THE FISH HOTEL
Buttermere
Via Cockermouth
Cumbria CA13 9XA
Tel: (017687) 70253

Mr and Mrs R H Knight
TREVENE
Buttermere
Via Cockermouth
Cumbria
Tel: (017687) 70210

Mrs L Norman
CRAGG FARM
Buttermere
Via Cockermouth
Cumbria CA13 9XA
Tel: (017687) 70204

Mrs A Kyle
SYKE FARM
Buttermere
Via Cockermouth
Cumbria CA13 9XA
Tel: (017687) 70222

STAGES: 5 & 6
Buttermere to
Braithwaite to
Portinscale

COLEDALE INN
Braithwaite
Nr Keswick
Cumbria CA12 5TN
Tel: (017687) 78272

Nick and Wendy Shill
IVY HOUSE HOTEL
Braithwaite
Nr Keswick
Cumbria CA12 5SY
Tel: (017687) 78338

Ian and Marion
Robinson
THELMLEA
Braithwaite.
Nr Keswick
Cumbria CA12 5TD
Tel: (017687) 78305

Chris White
APPLEGARTH GUEST
HOUSE
Braithwaite
Nr Keswick
Cumbria CA12 5TD
Tel: (017687) 78462

Mr and Mrs Wood
UZZICAR FARMHOUSE
Newlands
Nr Keswick
Cumbria CA12 5TS
Tel: (017687) 78239

Mrs M A Relph
LITTLETOWN FARM
Newlands
Nr Keswick
Cumbria CA12 5TU
Tel: (017687) 78353

STAGES: 6 & 7
Braithwaite to
Portinscale to
Threlkeld

Mrs J Davis
THE MOUNT
Portinscale
Nr Keswick
Cumbria CA12 5RD
Tel: (017687) 73070

Mr and Mrs J W
Holloway
DALGARTH HOUSE
Portinscale
Nr Keswick
Cumbria CA12 5RQ
Tel: (017687) 72817

Mrs M Seymour
POWE HOUSE
Portinscale
Nr Keswick
Cumbria CA12 5RW
Tel: (017687) 73611

Mike and Sue Newman
DERWENT COTTAGE
Portinscale
Nr Keswick
Cumbria CA12 5RF
Tel: (017687) 74838

Tim and Heather Tucker
ROOKING HOUSE
Portinscale
Nr Keswick
Cumbria CA12 5RD
Tel: (017687) 72506

Sue and Paul Trafford
THIRNBECK GUEST
HOUSE
Portinscale
Nr Keswick
Cumbria CA12 5RD
Tel: (017687) 72869

STAGES: 7 & 8
Portinscale to
Threlkeld to
Glenridding

Merle and Jim Wilson
HORSE AND FARRIER INN
Threlkeld
Nr Keswick
Cumbria CA12 4SQ
Tel: (017687) 79688

Mary and Jim Fearon
COBBLE RIGG
Threlkeld
Nr Keswick
Cumbria CA12 4SQ
Tel: (017687) 79743

Val and Paul Sunley
THE BUNGALOW,
SUNNYSIDE
Threlkeld
Nr Keswick
Cumbria CA12 4SD
Tel: (017687) 79679

Mrs E Hume
WOODEND
Threlkeld
Nr Keswick
Cumbria CA12 4SU
Tel: (017687) 79686

Anne Hughes
SADDLEBACK VIEW
Threlkeld
Nr Keswick
Cumbria
Tel: (017687) 79255

STAGES: 8 & 9
Threlkeld to
Glenridding to
Troutbeck

THE GLENRIDDING HOTEL
Glenridding, Ullswater
Nr Penrith
Cumbria CA11 0PB
Tel: (017684) 82228

John and Pauline Lake
MOSS CRAG
Glenridding, Ullswater
Nr Penrith
Cumbria CA11 0PA
Tel: (017684) 82500)

Jane Sharp
BRIDGE HOUSE
Glenridding, Ullswater
Nr Penrith
Cumbria CA11 0PA
Tel: (017684) 82236

Jane Clarke
BEECH HOUSE
Glenridding, Ullswater
Nr Penrith
Cumbria CA11 0PA
Tel: (017684) 82037

A M and L Pitchford
CHERRY HOLME
Square Hill
Glenridding, Ullswater
Nr Penrith
Cumbria CA11 0PF
Tel: (017684) 82512

Maureen Berryman
THE WHITE LION INN
Patterdale
Nr Penrith
Cumbria CA11 0NW
Tel: (017684) 82214

STAGES: 9 & 10
Glenridding to
Troutbeck to
Grasmere

Annette and
Christopher Poulsom
THE MORTAL MAN HOTEL
Troutbeck
Nr Windermere
Cumbria LA23 1PL
Tel: (015394) 33193

THE QUEEN'S HEAD
HOTEL
Troutbeck
Nr Windermere
Cumbria LA23 1PW
Tel: (015394) 32174

Mrs Maureen Evans
STAMP HOWE
Troutbeck
Nr Windermere
Cumbria LA23 1PL
Tel: (015394) 33136

Ruth and Roy Smith
SOUTH VIEW
Troutbeck
Nr Windermere
Cumbria LA23 1PH
Tel: (015394) 32026

Mrs Sally Simpson
HIGH FOLD FARM
Troutbeck
Nr Windermere
Cumbria LA23 1PG
Tel: (015394) 32200

APPENDIX: STATISTICS

TABLE 7 **SUMMARY OF TIME ALLOWANCES, DISTANCES WALKED AND HEIGHTS CLIMBED**

MAIN ROUTE

| Stage | Individual stages | | | | | Cumulative | | | | |
| | Time allow-ance | Distance walked (including height) | | Height climbed | | Time Allow-ance | Distance walked (including height) | | Height climbed | |
	Hours	Km	Miles	Metres	Feet	Hours	Km	Miles	Metres	Feet
1 GRASMERE to CONISTON	7.5	19.5	12.1	840	2750	7.5	19.5	12.1	840	2750
2 CONISTON to ELTERWATER	8.0	19.4	12.0	1210	3970	15.5	38.9	24.1	2050	6720
3 ELTERWATER to WASDALE HEAD	9.0	23.0	14.3	1540	5050	24.5	61.9	38.4	3590	11770
4 WASDALE HEAD to BUTTERMERE	8.0	17.8	11.1	1500	4920	32.5	79.7	49.5	5090	16690
5 BUTTERMERE to BRAITHWAITE	6.5	13.8	8.6	1100	3610	39.0	93.5	58.1	6190	20300
6 BRAITHWAITE to PORTINSCALE	9.0	24.3	15.1	1300	4270	48.0	117.8	73.2	7490	24570
7 PORTINSCALE to THRELKELD	7.5	20.8	13.0	1020	3350	55.5	138.6	86.2	8510	27920
8 THRELKELD to GLENRIDDING	8.0	20.6	12.8	1280	4200	63.5	159.2	99.0	9790	32120
9 GLENRIDDING to TROUTBECK	8.5	23.1	14.3	1140	3740	72.0	182.3	113.3	10930	35860
10 TROUTBECK to GRASMERE	8.0	20.9	13.0	1250	4100	80.0	203.2	126.3	12180	39960
	80.0	203.2	126.3	12180	39960					

EASIER ROUTE

| Stage | Individual stages | | | | | Cumulative | | | | |
| | Time allow-ance | Distance walked (including height) | | Height climbed | | Time Allow-ance | Distance walked (including height) | | Height climbed | |
	Hours	Km	Miles	Metres	Feet	Hours	Km	Miles	Metres	Feet
1 GRASMERE to CONISTON	6.5	17.5	10.9	600	1970	6.5	17.5	10.9	600	1970
2 CONISTON to ELTERWATER	7.0	16.1	10.0	950	3120	13.5	33.6	20.9	1550	5090
3 ELTERWATER to WASDALE HEAD	7.5	19.2	11.9	1120	3670	21.0	52.8	32.8	2670	8760
4 WASDALE HEAD to BUTTERMERE	5.0	11.1	6.9	670	2200	26.0	63.9	39.7	3340	10960
5 BUTTERMERE to BRAITHWAITE	5.0	10.3	6.4	670	2200	31.0	74.2	46.1	4010	13160
6 BRAITHWAITE to PORTINSCALE	7.0	18.8	11.7	780	2560	38.0	93.0	57.8	4790	15720
7 PORTINSCALE to THRELKELD	7.0	18.2	11.3	960	3150	45.0	111.2	69.1	5750	18870
8 THRELKELD to GLENRIDDING	6.5	16.7	10.4	900	2950	51.5	127.9	79.5	6650	21820
9 GLENRIDDING to TROUTBECK	6.5	17.4	10.8	620	2030	58.0	145.3	90.3	7270	23850
10 TROUTBECK to GRASMERE	6.0	13.5	8.4	870	2860	64.0	158.8	98.7	8140	26710
	64.0	158.8	98.7	8140	26710					

TABLE 8 **PRINCIPAL FELLS INDICATING THOSE CLIMBED**

Fell	Height (per OS Maps etc.)		Stage		
	Metres	Feet	Main	Main (Optional extension)	Easier
Fells over 3000 feet					
1 Scafell Pike	978	3210	3		3
2 Scafell	964	3162			
3 Helvellyn	950	3118	8		
4 Broad Crag	945	3100		3	
5 Ill Crag	935	3070		3	
6 Skiddaw	931	3053	7		7
7 Lower Man (Helvellyn)	925	3033	8		
Fells between 2501 and 3000 feet					
8 Great End	910	2984		3	
9 Bow Fell	902	2960	3		
10 Great Gable	899	2949		4	
11 Pillar	892	2927	4		
12 Nethermost Pike	891	2920		8	
13 Catstye Cam	890	2917		8	
14 Esk Pike	885	2903	3		
15 Raise	883	2889	8		
16 Fairfield	873	2863	10		
17 Blencathra (Saddleback)	868	2847			
18 Little Man (Skiddaw)	865	2837			
19 White Side	863	2832	8		
20 Crinkle Crags	859	2816	3		
21 Dollywaggon Pike	858	2810		8	
22 Great Dodd	857	2807	8		8
23 Grasmoor	852	2791	5		
24 Stybarrow Dodd	843	2770	8		8
25 Scoat Fell	841	2760			
26 St Sunday Crag	841	2756			
27 Crag Hill	839	2749		5	
28 High Street	828	2718	9		
29 Red Pike (Wastwater)	826	2707			
30 Hart Crag	822	2698	10		
31 Steeple	819	2687			
32 Lingmell	807	2649		3	
33 High Stile	806	2644		4	
34 Coniston Old Man	803	2635	2		2

continued

PRINCIPAL FELLS INDICATING THOSE CLIMBED – cont.

Fell	Height (per OS Maps etc.)		Stage		
	Metres	Feet	Main	Main (Optional extension)	Easier
Fells between 2501 and 3000 feet – continued					
35 High Raise (Haweswater)	802	2634			
36 Kirk Fell	802	2630		4	
37 Swirl How (Coniston Fells)	802	2630	2		2
38 Green Gable	801	2628			
39 Haycock	797	2618			
40 Brim Fell	796	2611			
41 Dove Crag	792	2603	10		
42 Grisedale Pike	791	2593	5		
43 Watson's Dodd	789	2584	8		8
44 Rampsgill Head	792	2581			
45 Great Carrs	785	2575		2	2
46 Allen Crags	785	2572			
47 Thornthwaite Crag	784	2569	9		
48 Glaramara	781	2560			
49 Kidsty Pike	780	2560		9	
50 Dow Crag	778	2555	2		
51 Red Screes	776	2541			
52 Harter Fell (Mardale)	778	2539		9	
53 Grey Friar	773	2536		2	
54 Wandope	772	2533			
55 Sail	773	2530		5	
56 Hopegill Head	770	2525	5		
57 Great Rigg	766	2513	10		
58 Stony Cove Pike	763	2502			
59 Wetherlam	762	2502	2		

INDEX